Black People White People

Who is the Devil?

By Rasheed L. Muhammad

Revised Edition 2013

Copyright © 2009 All Rights Reserved

Made in USA

Introduction

The subject of race has been a thorn in the side of many Americans, mainly between what we call black people and white people. One hardly ever sees a public debate hashed out by Korean Americans, Mexican Americas, Native Americans, Japanese Americans, (in other words, Brown, Red and Yellow people) over how white people mistreat them. Of course, other "races" suffer discrimination under white America's America. But no other two people *butt heads* about race more then black and white.

What is the difference between ethnic conflicts and racial conflicts? For the most part, *"black skin people"* and *"white skin"* peoples' conflict is not wholly about race. It's more about the institutional, political, and economic factors, and those whom govern them; namely, white people! In other words, it's more about control because control equals power and those in power represent the authority figures— *"the deciders."* This is the reason Europeans make war against Europeans, Africans make war against Africans, Middle Easterners make war against Middle Easterners and so forth. Someone is fighting for authority. The difference however is that when you live among hundreds and millions of other people who look like you in skin tone and then conflicts arise, such fights are perhaps ethnic or personal. But in America, most are led to believe black and white conflicts are solely race based simply because of skin color differences.

The friendship between black people and white people is just beneath the surface of a smile, a facial twitch, a voice tone and a wink of the eye. It is based more on idle talk, gossip, sport and play. The question is why and the answer is easy....HISTORY!

The legacy of slavery in North America and white superiority from 1619 to 1965 is a disgrace. It's no wonder the Biblical story of the Israelites illustrate how they were separated from their former slave masters and given some land of their own. I imagine after serving Pharaoh 400 years, their chances of getting justice, peace and equality from their former slave masters was slim to very slim. Therefore, they needed a land of their own. Likewise, African Americans; also former slaves of the American Government, have given their all to make themselves socially acceptable to white America's value systems' through processes of *accommodation* and *assimilation*. Yet, enmity between black and white remains firm just beneath the surface of a smile or hello.

Many educated and wealthy black *individuals* have constructed new knowledge from their experiences as international citizens of the world and incorporated their new experiences into an already existing framework dominated and controlled; too often, by somebody with white skin. These Black upwardly mobile men and women have grown to understand the institutional, political, and economic ramifications behind the white power structure to which they do not control. So it's not about race. What Blacks seek is more institutional, political, economic and judicial authority in the land where their ancestors were once slaves. And this, my friend, white America comprehends, but cannot accommodate to the satisfaction of black America.

Over past 600 years, the Caucasian civilization was able to reshape the ancient worldview and now rule 186 nations through the International Monetary Fund, World Bank and Industrial Military Complex apparatus. Their financial oppression and unbalanced global police policy is at root of what is called the race problem, especially in North America.

For Black America, her solution to the race problem is really determined when its power elites stop mealy mouthing around on television broadcast as not to lose their nearness to white folks; deal first and foremost amongst them with an eye on institutional, political, economic and judicial equity. Once this stance is intelligently enthroned, all real adversaries will be made manifest. Afterwards, the race problem may be capsulated because black on black U.S. ethnic conflict is the great problem to resolve! Let us not forget the words of the Most Honorable Elijah Muhammad who said in 1973:

> *"Our slave-masters' children have reared our fathers and mothers to be enemies of each other. They have destroyed our love of self and kind. They have educated us to hate and refuse all that goes for Black people. This lack of love for self and kind keeps us divided, and being divided we are a nation of prey at the hands of our ever open enemies.*
>
> *"Whatever the amount of education we receive from our enemies we are still the slaves of our enemies due to this lack of knowledge of self, God and the devil; the true religion; self-pride; self-interest; and self-independence and the desire of a country and of a government of our own under the law of justice and righteousness for every one of our poor Black people throughout the earth. But let us start first here in America where we are the victims of no freedom, justice and equality and we know the pains of being divided.*
>
> *"At present, we have hundreds of clubs and organizations; thousands of scholars, hundreds of educators, scientists, technicians, doctors, lawyers, judges, congressmen, ambassadors, professors, tradesmen of all kinds and engineers of most every kind. We have all kinds of religious believers, teachers, and preachers by the thousands, agriculturists, herdsmen and hundreds of hunters of wild game. What more do we need but unity of the whole for the whole? What actually is preventing this unity… is the ignorance and foolish love and fear of our enemies in the professional and leadership class of…Black people up from slavery.*

"There are disgraceful "Uncle Toms" in a world of freedom, learning and advanced science in every branch of study. How long shall we seek the white men's education to become their servants instead of becoming builders of a progressive nation of our own on some of this earth that we can call our own?"[1]

There are many whites who are ready to see a better world come into existence and know legal injustice and debt financing cannot adequately revitalize 40 to 60 million black Americans, not to speak of the 103 million white Americans and other races. They know blacks are not a threatening force against America nor do blacks desire to destroy America. By design, America's former slaves and their offspring have the nature to lead a world called heaven on earth for all people regardless of race, color or creed. Once they are enthroned with institutional, political, economic and judicial equity, without interference from the old white world order, a new government can emerge and racial tensions shall diminish. Essentially, the root cause of America's racial issue is grave ignorance, greed and scarcity minds. This little book was written to uncover such ignorance. It searches out the origin of what power prepared Caucasian civilization as vicegerents over world affairs, how they got into West Asia 6,000 years ago, out of the caves of the Caucus palisade in 4,000 BC and the scientific genetic differences between blacks and whites.

You want to talk about a humbling experience. Read *"Black People White People Who Is The Devil?"* in its entirety. Just as 400 years of slavery, suffering and death produced a truth in the minds of African Americans to desire a better world, the unadulterated message of this book was designed to relent the same affect in the mind of Caucasians about from whence they came and why they were empowered to disrupt peace (Islam) among aboriginal nations and cities, in particular, over the past 6,000 years.

---

[1] http://www.muhammadspeaks.com/disputetruth.html

"If Islam had been forced upon all the people of the earth during the past 6,000 years there would not have been any 'world of Christianity,' there would not have been any 'World of Buddhism...and there would never have been anything like 'The Caucasian World.' Islam would have prevented their progress. God Himself has held Islam 'in check' to give these other 'worlds' free reign during the past 6,000 years." [2]

In the very near future, the Caucasian World's institutional, political, economic and judicial maintenance over the earth will become a memory of the past. Their future, as individuals, partly depends upon whether they can stand up and declare themselves proud members of the original black nation and bow down to the One True Living God whose proper name is Allah!

---

[2] (Elijah Muhammad Dec. 1960 (Vol. 1, No. 4) edition of Muhammad Speaks Newspaper)

Table of Content

ONE 11

Genetic Makeup of the White Race 11
TWO 21

Is the White Race the Devil 21
THREE 27

The Real Caveman 27
   Quranic History 18:94-100 33
FOUR 35

Black Man Of Ancient Europe 35
FIVE 43

Mediterranean Caucasoid 43
   Western Semitic People In Central Asia and Musasir 45
   Homeland of Early Civilized Whites 48
   Iran 50
SIX 59

Mountain Jews 59
   Zoroastrianism 62
   People of The Book's Pseudepigrapha 63
   Bible is Deluted 64
SEVEN 73

Nimrod Ruins Moses' Civilization 73
   The Winged Ones 75
   Nimrod Married His Mother 78
   Moses' Temple Attack 84

EIGHT **87**

Skunk Of The Planet Earth **87**
   Battle In the Sky.. 90
Appendix 1.. **100**
   Failure Of The Turks.. 100
Appendix 2.. **104**
   List of Prophets Over Past 6,000 Years 104
Appendix 3.. **109**
   Pkharmat 109
   Other Books by the Author 111

ONE
Genetic Makeup of the White Race

The word "gene" is often used to refer to the hereditary *cause* of a human trait. Genes also determine ones skin color. Skin color can range from almost black to pinkish white in different people. Skin color is determined by the amount and type of the pigment melanin in the skin.

Melanin comes in two types: phaeomelanin (red to yellow) and eumelanin (dark brown to black). Both amount and type are determined by 4-6 genes which operate under what is called incomplete dominance. Each gene comes in several combinations resulting in a great variety of different skin colors. Basically one has either dominate traits (*AA*), incomplete dominate traits (*Aa*) or recessive traits (*aa*).

With respect to the genetic nature of white or pink skin people, this is indicative of the recessive gene (*aa*). Black skin is indicative of the dominant gene (*AA*); and Brown, Red and Yellow are indicative of the incomplete dominant gene (*Aa*). Today no intelligent person argues over the fact that all people derive from Black skin men and women of the earth.

In the study of molecular evolution, a **haplogroup represents the relationship each ethnic group has with a common ancestor—Asiatic black nation**.

In human genetics, **Haplogroup A** (M91) is a Y-chromosome haplogroup. Haplogroup A is found mainly in the Southern Nile region and Southern Africa. It represents the oldest and most diverse of the human Y-chromosome haplogroups. It is believed to be the haplogroup corresponding to Y-chromosomal Adam.

Haplogroup G (M201) is a Y-chromosome haplogroup most frequent in the Caucasus (found at over

60% in ethnic North Ossetian males and around 30% in Georgian males). The Kabardinian and Balkarian peoples of the northwestern Caucasus are known to be 29% G. Armenians are known to have around 11% of their males in HgG. The exceptionally high level of G in the North Ossetians has attracted attention and speculation. Since the Ossetians trace their descent from the Alans it was thought that the Alans and their presumed ancestors the Scythians must also have been high in Haplogroup G. **Haplogroup I** represents nearly one-fifth of the population of Europe.[3]

"The Alans [ancient ancestors the Ossetia Caucus Mountain tribe], an ancient nomadic pastoral people that occupied the steppe region northeast of the Black Sea. The Alani were first mentioned in Roman literature in the 1st century ad and were described later as a warlike people that specialized in horse breeding. They frequently raided the Parthian [Iranian] empire and the Caucasian provinces of the Roman Empire. About 370 AD, however, they were overwhelmed by the Huns, and many fled westward, crossing into Gaul with the Vandals and Suebi in 406 AD. Although some of the Alani settled near Orléans and Valence, most went to North Africa with the Vandals, causing the official title of the Vandal kings in Africa to be "kings of the Vandals and the Alani." The Alani who remained under the rule of the Huns are said to be ancestors of the modern Ossetes of the Caucasus."[4]

Overall haplogroups run the gamet from A to Z with many branches, sub-branches and mutations. But they all are ancestors of the Original Black nation's gene pool. This is why the Bible {*Acts 17:26*} reads, *"From one man he made every nation of men, that they should inhabit the whole earth; and he determined the times set for them and the*

---

[3] http://en.wikipedia.org/wiki/Haplogroup
[4] www.britannica.com/EBchecked/topic/12171/Alani

White People

exact places where they should live." The point here is that all other races derive from the father of civilization, the Black man and women of the earth (Africa and Asia).

The question becomes how the white did or pink skin people get into civilization. Dr. Dr. C. George Boeree exclaims:

> *"The experts are pretty much in agreement about how the varieties of skin color came about. They suggest that prehumans were likely white with fur - just like our relatives, the chimpanzees. As our hair became thinner, melanin came to the rescue to protect us from the sun's damaging ultraviolet rays. We became a brown people as our whiter relations died of skin cancer or from a lack of the B vitamin folate, which is needed for DNA synthesis, and without which we see more birth defects. Some people in Africa even evolved dark black skin."[5]*

The Honorable Elijah Muhammad revealed:

> *"It was a black man by the name of Yakub, 6,600 years ago who grafted the white race out of us. They are from us. They have tried to cover their birth and their father and their mother by saying that they came from sea life; then, if they came from sea life, then sea life is their god, or their father; or that they're from animals [apes]. They would rather say that most anything is their god, other than to say a black man was their god."[6]*

Mr. Muhammad furthermore goes on to reveal:

> *"We have been ruled by the white race for the past 6,000 years. Whether or not they actually ruled all of the 6,000 years, it was given to them! In the beginning of their creation they had the rights and the authority from Almighty Allah and the scientist in that day to rule us for 6,000 years... They were run out from among the Holy people and were punished for 2,000 years without any guide. They have not that history nor have you been given it. What went on 2,000 years before Moses' birth. They take up for Moses. They had two great prophets during their last 4,000 years, Moses and Jesus. They have not*

---

[5] http://webspace.ship.edu/cgboer/race.html
[6] http://www.muhammadspeaks.com/Evolution.html

believed in either one! They have not practiced the religion of either one! The last 4,000 years we have had many religions other than Islam. We have had many representatives of God representing this and that. Wood, Iron, Gold, Silver, Monkeys, everything has been worshipped! Cows have been worshipped as God."[7]

Map 1 on the next page sites Caucasoid known savage tribal names. Map 2 on page 16 provides modern names of Caucasoid tribes whom survived their great movements out chaos into monarchy. Truth of the matter is: white people or Caucasians are the youngest race among all others produced from the incomplete dominant (Aa) gene.

Whereas the Original Man is Self-Created, the made man (white race) derives from **sex** between members of the original nation. Thus the reason they were identified with the number 6. *"Here is wisdom. Let him that hath understanding **count the number of the beast: for it is the number of a man; and his number [is] Six hundred threescore [and] six."** (Revelation 13:18)* The man there is the original Black nation, who were not perfect themselves and the beast represents the nature and cruel actions of the Caucasian civilization in terms of their ruling techniques employed to rule the original nations of the earth. Not every single individual equally cruel, yet by nature wicked. That was 6,600 years ago they were made by the somatic law of 4-6 genes operating within the *incomplete dominance gene* pool of **Haplogroup A**—eumelanin (dark brown to black). As it were, from these original black human beings, a recessive man contrary to the original was grafted into civilization.

> *"Let us make man in our image, after our likeness: and let them have dominion over the fish of the sea, and over the fowl of the air, and over the cattle, and over all the earth, and over every creeping thing that creepeth upon the earth." (Genesis 1:26)*

---

[7] http://www.muhammadspeaks.com/6000YearHistory.html

White People

Map - 1 Ancient Map and Tribal Names

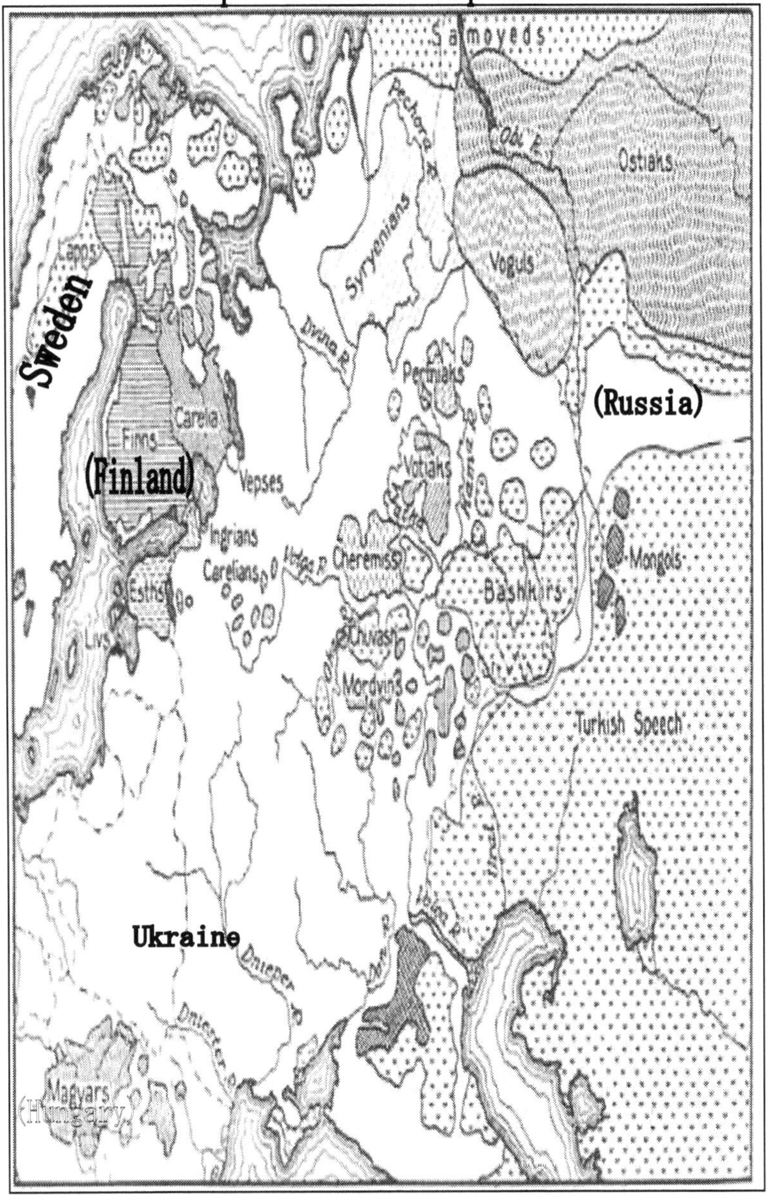

www.friendsofsabbath.org/Further_Research/e-books/Races of Europe - C Coon/chapter-IX8.htm

Map 2 - Modern Map and Tribal Names

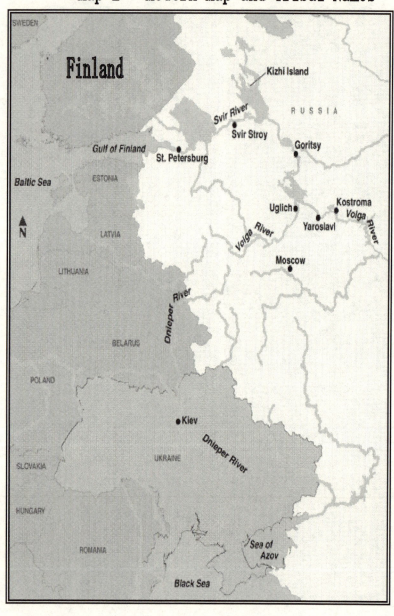

White People

Lastly, the Honorable Elijah Muhammad reveals:

"... the father (Yakub) discovered in the germ of the Black man that a brown germ was there also. And he made a white person through grafting from the brown germ. This made the made-man unalike from the self-created man (the Black man). The Black man is self-created, while white mankind is a made-man by experimenting with the germs and ideas of the maker. The idea of the maker was to make one to rule the original Black man (who is self-created and has no birth record of his creation). He had to make him an unalike man of the original man. Therefore, he grafted his made-man unalike. He knew the science of unalike attracts while alike repels.

"IN OUR 25-thousand-year cycle of making history for our Nation, there was a vacuum of 6,000 years. This Yakub, the father of the white man, was aware of. Therefore, he put his made-man in the vacuum to rule. This vacuum extended from the 9,000th year to the 15,000th year of our calendar history, so God (in the Person of Master Fard Muhammad) to whom praises are due forever, taught me. His making the made-man unalike to attract alike was a perfect job. He foresaw the end of the unalike made-man, and was perfect in knowledge that this type man could rule alike (the original man). Therefore, Mr. Yakub's idea became a fruitful one. He would make a man an enemy to his original self and kind, (Yakub was an original man.) This made-man's wisdom had no permanence and would be limited to the coming of an alike person to take over his way of rule.

"The original God is our father, but not the father of the white man. The white man is made by an enemy of ours who seized upon the chance to put an enemy to rule us into the opposite of our nature (righteousness). The only way he could get us to listen to such a made-man for 6,000 years was that he had to make him unalike. He had to make him with something to attract us. SO OUR fathers of 6,000 years ago (the original Black man of Arabia) saw this unalike person emerging from the Island of the Aegean Sea and were attracted by this people----so much so that they began to take them as friends

and even to marry them and hide them away in their homes. They had been attracted by an unalike person. They had never seen a white human being before. He was not made in Arabia but he was made out of Arabia on an Island in the sea. He was not allowed to be made in the Holy Land. As the Bible teaches us, when Yakub's knowledge or idea of making the made-man was discovered they cast him and those who believed with him out (you will find this in Genesis) where it reads: 'Drive him out lest he put his hand on the tree of life and live forever.'[8]

The chart below shows how the **6 incomplete dominate genes** possesses the potential to transmit a 100% recessive race by pairing sex partners.

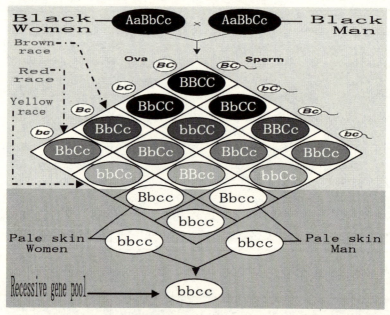

A recessive gene pool will never produce a Black skin person! The Honorable Elijah Muhammad revealed that it took 600 years to extract a white skin or pink skin or recessive gene person from the Black dominant gene person. The key was to prevent mating between black with

---

[8] http://www.muhammadspeaks.com/Unalikeattracts4-5-1968.html

black and only allow Black to brown, then brown with brown. Then brown to yellow, then yellow with yellow, which ultimately produced white skin or pink skin (recessive gene) people by nature. He said this type of experiment occurred on the Island of Pelan (Patmos) in the Aegean Sea 6,600 years ago. Interestingly enough, it was this race of people whom Ancient Egyptians once upon a time classified as Sea People.

During these modern times, the ultimate example of a recessive gene carrier is demonstrated when a child is born with blue eyes, blond hair and pale skin. It never seems to amaze parents whose child is born as such and then gradually their eyes may turn green or brown, hair turn red or brunette and skin turns more toned. Reason being, the dominant genes are dominating over the recessive genes.

"Remember that Black, by itself, is no color. It is original. It is not from any other color. It is durable in any climate of the earth and it remains the same."
[Quote by the Honorable Elijah Muhammad]

In conclusion, without the presence of the original Black nation, there would not be a *"white or pale skin"* population on the earth. The leaders of the pale skin race were once referred to as "people of the book or scripture." It was written in advance that a new genetically made race would rule the world for a short time.

TWO
Is the White Race the Devil

The French poet Charles Baudelaire, once said, *"The greatest trick the Devil ever pulled was convincing the world he didn't exist."* (Feb. 1864, The Generous Gambler)

Modern conceptions of the Devil include the concept that it symbolizes humans 'own lower nature or sinfulness. In mainstream Christianity, God and the Devil are usually portrayed as fighting over the souls of humans, with the Devil seeking to lure people away from God and into Sheol (hell). As God commands a force of human believers to carry out His will, likewise the Devil commands a force of humans to carry out his will. The Hebrew Bible (or Old Testament) describes the Adversary (Ha-satan) as a servant of God whose job it is to test humankind. Many other religions have a trickster or tempter figure that is similar to the Devil. For instance, Zoroastrianism, one the world's oldest recorded monotheistic religions assigns the term lie or decay or chaos as the adversary to creation and not necessary an entity.

The name *'Devil'* derives from the Greek word *diabolos*, which means *'slanderer'* or *'accuser'*. In law, **defamation** (also called **calumny**, **libel** (for written words), **slander** (for spoken words), and **vilification** is the communication of a statement that makes a claim, expressly stated or implied to be factual, that may give an individual, business, product, group, government or nation a negative image. It is usually, but not always, a requirement that this claim be false and that the publication is communicated to someone other than the person defamed (the claimant).[9]

---

[9] http://en.wikipedia.org/wiki/Defamation

For example, in 1787 the United States Government by law defamed, libeled, vilified and slandered its African slaves as three-fifths human. *U.S.* law made its calumnious claim to be factual by writing and framing Article 1, Section 2, Paragraph 3 of the United States Constitution in the following words:

> "Representatives and direct Taxes shall be apportioned among the several States which may be included within this Union, according to their respective Numbers, which shall be determined by adding to the whole Number of free Persons, including those bound to Service for a Term of Years, and excluding Indians not taxed, three fifths of all other Persons."

In common law jurisdictions, slander refers to a malicious, false and defamatory *spoken* statement or report, while libel refers to any other form of communication such as *written* words or images. Most jurisdictions allow legal actions, civil and/or criminal, to deter various kinds of defamation and retaliate against groundless criticism. Point and case: human devils draw these images to libel Black America!

In effect, Article 1, Section 2, Paragraph 3 of the United States Constitution gave Caucasian Christians a legal right to hold slaves and profit handsomely. There slanderous Article was framed to justify ill-gotten profits, trade and wealth with and from other European governments. During these modern times, however, men and women on an individual basis express their slander as they please. If certain legal lines are crossed regarding defamation or slander, a court hearing commences. And as it should be, the victim of such crimes may likewise be rewarded handsomely. My point is: The Devil can be a man, a race and/or a government system conducted by men and women with lower natures.

However, when a government acts as the Devil, like the United States Government (under Caucasian rule) did against its African slaves, how shall this matter be adjudicated? Abraham Lincoln said in his debates with Stephen Douglas in 1858:

> *"I am not, nor ever have been, in favor of bringing about in any way the social and political equality of the white and black races, that I am not nor ever have been in favor of making voters or jurors of negroes, nor of qualifying them to hold office, nor to intermarry with white people; and I will say in addition to this that there is a physical difference between the white and black races which I believe will forever forbid the two races living together on terms of social and political equality. And inasmuch as they cannot so live, while they do remain together there must be the position of superior and inferior and I as much as any other man am in favor of having the superior position assigned to the white race."*

It appears Lincoln was more interested in retaining the power of the Caucasian Government rather than freeing the slaves. Therefore, the criminal act behind Article 1, Section 2, Paragraph 3 of the United States Constitution and the slanderous three-fifth compromise framed by white America's doctors of law and religious leaders scientifically made Caucasians fit the identity of Devil. I reiterate, their legal false promotion of Africans in America as $3/5^{th}$ of a human being was about greed, trade, wealth and apportionment of taxes levied against the states. Overall, it was all about "In God We Trust"...money!

James Madison is credited with drafting the 3/5th's compromised upon which southern and northern states would agree how to classify Blacks. Their general consensus meant that it was a necessary evil. But they never reveal why it was a necessary evil.

James Madison

It's not a wonder why abolitionist eventually raised the idea to end slavery, perchance they might rid America's Christian nation of such a scourge of God's divine judgment. Notwithstanding, there is no justification for centuries of American style slave trading practices. They were forewarned to end slavery almost from the beginning of the 13 colonies by a very wise man sent to them from Europe's elite class. His name was Francis Daniel Pastorius, Attorney at law.

> "The **1688 Germantown Quaker Petition Against Slavery** was the first protest against African American slavery made by a religious body in the English colonies. It was drafted **by Francis Daniel Pastorius** and signed by him and three other Quakers living in Germantown, Pennsylvania (now part of Philadelphia) on behalf of the Germantown Meeting of **the Religious Society of Friends**. It was forwarded to the monthly, quarterly, and yearly meetings without any action being taken on it. According to John Greenleaf Whittier, the original document was discovered in 1844 by the Philadelphia antiquarian Nathan Kite and published in The Friend (Vol. XVIII. No. 16)."[10]

Francis D. Pastorius

The Honorable Elijah Muhammad revealed on page 59 of his book *Message To The Blackman*: "According to the word of Allah (God) and the history of the world, since the grafting of the Caucasian race 6,000 years ago, they have caused more bloodshed than any people known to the black nation. Born murderers, their very nature is to murder. The

---

[10] http://www.ushistory.org/germantown/people/pastorius.htm

Bible and Holy Quran Sharrieff are full of teachings of this bloody race of devils. They shed the life blood of all life, even their own, and are scientists at deceiving the black people.

"They deceived the very people of Paradise (Bible, Gen. 3:13). They killed their own brother (Gen. 4:8). The innocent earth's blood (Gen. 4:10) revealed it to its Maker (thy brother's blood cried unto me from the ground). The very earth, the soil of America, soaked with the innocent blood of the so-called Negroes shed by this race of devils, now cried out to its Maker for her burden of carrying the innocent blood of the righteous slain upon her. Let us take a look at the devil's creation from the teaching of the Holy Quran. *'And when your Lord said to the angels, I am going to place in the earth one who shall rule, the angels said: What will Thou place in it such as shall make mischief in it and shed blood, we celebrate Thy praise and extol Thy holiness (Holy Quran Sharrieff 2:30).*

"This devil race has and still is doing just that -- making mischief and shedding blood of the black nation whom they were grafted from. Your Lord said to the angels, *'Surely I am going to create a mortal of the essence of black mud fashioned in shape'. (Holy Quran Sharrieff, 15:28).* The essence of black mud (the black nation) mentioned is only symbolic, which actually means the sperm of the black nation, and they refused to recognize the black nation as their equal though they were made from and by a black scientist (named Yakub). They can never see their way in submitting to Allah and the religion Islam and His prophets."

For delivering this type of message, Elijah Muhammad was called a hate teacher. Especially during the 1960's at the apex of America's black and white racial wars. The great travesty; however, between these two people is that as long as Black people conduct themselves in acquiescence as not to appear bold over their white counterparts, everyone can get along. But when whites perceive and/or are made to feel otherwise, well…you must know the rest of the story.

"In the [Bible] parable of the donkey who balked upon meeting with the angel, the donkey saw that the burden he had been carrying on his back was false (Baal). So, in the Resurrection of the mentally dead so-called Negro, they are rising to the knowledge of self. This knowledge makes the so-called Negro to balk or refuse to continue carrying the slave-master as something of worship. This balking has angered the slave-master as the donkey's refusal angered Baal. Baal set about whipping and beating the donkey to force him as usual to carry and respect him as his master. This use of force to compel the once-slave (the Black Americans) to remain with them even now in order to make them members of their society is only false recognition of the Black man in America-this lost and now-found people of the Black Nation of Asia and Africa.

"England and America dislike the idea of having Allah dispose of their power over the so-called Negro, though they knew this was coming (the loss of their slaves) " [11]

---

[11] http://www.muhammadspeaks.com/HellErupts.html

THREE
The Real Caveman

Caucasians have defeated every ethnic group outside of Europe over the past 600 years in the name of Jesus Christ; under the symbol of the cross. Their proclaimed agenda was to civilize all native peoples from the Polynesian Islands to the jungles of Brazil and West Africa. Of course there were other aboriginals (living beyond the centre of the holy land's institutionalized government systems) who were also Hellenized and Christianized especially after 1492. But before achieving their global ends, Caucasians had to first fight amongst themselves while in Europe. The victors ultimately represented a combination of Western and Eastern European tribes who now govern together as best they can to hold up their world till its breaking point—the final world war between east and west.

Europe's unique race of people directly ties them to the palisades of the Caucus Mountain Range. There they dwelled 2000 solid years. Altogether, it took another 700 years until all were  clean enough and civil enough to exit the caves. Holy Quran 18:25, *"So they stayed in their Cave Three hundred years, and (some) Add nine (more)".* From this point, they began entering the southern hemisphere of central Asia, Asia Minor and even down into Southern Europe—Roman Italy.

In Book IV, Xenophon Anbasis mentions the underground tunnels having been used in the Caucasus Mountains. Xenophon Anabasis goes on to say that the white inhabitants once shared those tunnels with 'goat, sheep, cattle, fowls, and their young' and were reared and took their fodder. The suggestion is that in order to protect the animals from theft, it was necessary to keep them underground. In Prehistoric Antiquities of the Aryan Peoples, Dr. O. Schrader also discusses the ancient use of 'subterranean dwellings', i.e., dwellings dug in the earth, the existence of which is recorded amongst numerous Indo Germanic peoples, and which afforded protection against the summer's heat and the winter's cold. So the fact that after they arrived in the hills of West Asia the whites was compelled to seek refuge in the caves.[12] Quranic chapter 18 gave eastern world Muslims insight into the origin and great future of the Caucasian race (later called Christians and Jews) and how they would one day become rulers over the entire world of nations.

> *"15. 'Here are our people setting up gods beside Him. If only they could provide any proof to support their stand! Who is more evil than the one who fabricates lies and attributes them to GOD?'... 19. When we resurrected them, they asked each other, 'How long have you been here?' 'We have been here one day or part of the day,' they answered. 'Your Lord knows best how long we stayed here, so let us send one of us with this money to the city. Let him fetch the cleanest food, and buy some for us. Let him keep a low profile, and attract no attention. 20. 'If they discover you, they will stone you, or force you to revert to their religion, then you can never succeed.' 21. We caused them to be discovered, to let everyone know that GOD's promise is true, and to remove all doubt concerning the end of the world..."* (Holy Quran 18:15; 19-21)

The Holy Quran mystically reveals that Zul-Qarnain conferred with a specific group of people whom we now identify as *people of the book*—Christians and Jews. Moses (Mossa) is the name used to identify the prophet whom Allah first sent to civilize and help Caucasians create their chief nation. And so it was those who were first civilized by Mossa that later requested protection from Zul-Qarneyn to police the other savage tribes left within Iberie (palisades of the

---

[12] Making of the Whiteman, by Paul Lawrence Guthrie pg. 80.

White People

Caucus). *"They said: O Dhu'l-Qarneyn! Lo! Gog and Magog are spoiling the land. So may we pay thee tribute on condition that thou set a barrier between us and them?"* {18:94} **Map 3** below shows **Iberie**—the **palisade** mentioned in Quran—the area where Yacub's grafted race were originally sent 6,000 years ago, confined 2,000 years and set at liberty in 4,000 BC by the proverbial Moses (Mossa).

Map 3

I added the Jewish symbol representing two famous historical ancient Jewish settlements to the west and east, outside of the Caucus Iberie palisade.

www.columbia.edu/itc/mealac/pritchett/00generallinks/mallet/turkey/ancientalbania1...

"83. They ask you about Zul-Qarnain. Say, 'I will narrate to you some of his history.' 84. We [نَحْنُ nahnu] granted him authority on earth, and provided him with all kinds of means. 85. Then, he pursued one way. 86. When he reached the far west [**Urartu, Trans-Caucus Region**], *he found the sun setting in a vast ocean, and found people there. We said, 'O Zul-Qarnain, you can rule as you wish; either punish, or be kind to them.' 87. He said, 'As for those who transgress, we will punish them; then, when they return to their Lord, He will commit them to more retribution. 88. 'As for those who believe and lead a righteous life, they receive a good reward; we will treat them kindly.' 89. Then he pursued another way. 90. Until, when he reached the (land of) the rising sun* **[Indus]**, *he found it rising on a people to whom We had given no shelter from it -- 91. Naturally, we were fully aware of everything he found out. 92. He then pursued another way. 93. When he reached the valley between two palisades* **[Central Russian Plains of the Sarmatie]**, *he found people whose language was barely understandable. 94. They said, 'O Zul-Qarnain, Gog and Magog are corruptors of the earth."*

Who is Zul-Qarnain? His identity has been a controversial matter from the earliest times. It is my opinion the word Zul-Qarnain represents a title, meaning ruler or king. Many Islamic commentators said he was Alexander the Great.

> *"The Gates of Alexander are most commonly identified with the Caspian Gates of Derbent (Russia) whose thirty north-looking towers used to stretch for forty kilometers between the Caspian Sea and the Caucasus Mountains, effectively blocking the passage across the Caucasus.*
>
> *"Although the current fortifications date to well after Alexander's death, some scholars postulate that there might have been earlier fortifications built during the Achaemenid Persian Empire (the area has indeed been settled for at least 5000 years). If this is true, agents of Alexander's empire may have visited or even strengthened them after the Achaemenids were conquered, though Alexander personally never travelled that far north.*

> *"In the Alexander Romance, Alexander chases his enemies to a pass between two peaks in the Caucasus known as the 'Breasts of the World'. He decides to imprison the 'unclean nations' of the north, which include Gog and Magog, behind a huge wall of steel or adamantine. With the aid of God, Alexander and his men close the narrow pass, keeping the uncivilized Gog and Magog from pillaging the peaceful southern lands.*[13]

On the other hand, some Islamic and Jewish commentators are inclined to believe Zul-Qarnain was Cyrus of Bible, an ancient Achaemenid king of Persia (modern day Iran).

> *"The first characteristics applicable to Cyrus, for according to the Bible Prophet Daniel saw in his vision that the united kingdom of Media and Persia was like a two-horned ram before the rise of the Greeks. (**Dan. 8: 3,"20**). The Jews had a very high opinion of 'The Two-horned' one, because it was his invasion, which brought about the downfall of the kingdom of Babylon and the liberation of the Israelites...*
>
> *"Historically it is enough to say that Cyrus was a Persian ruler, whose rise began about 549 B.C. In a few years, he conquered the kingdom of Media and Lydia and afterwards conquered Babylon in 539 B.C. After this no powerful kingdom was left to oppose him. His conquests extended to Sind and the territory known as Turkistan on one side, and to Egypt and Libya and to Thrace and Macedonia and to Caucasia and Khawarzam in the North. In fact, the whole civilized world was under his sway."* [14]

This history moreover refers to 539 BC when the Achaemenid Persian king, Cyrus, subdued Babylon, freed the Israelites (or *people of the book* as they were once classified by the ancients) and then allowed them to return to Jerusalem from Assyrian controlled Babylon. Did all leave, No, some Jewish Rabbi's remained in Babylon.

Nevertheless, after the demise of Prophet Mohammed of Arabia in 632 AD, his followers decided to

---

[13] (Source) Wikipedia, the free encyclopedia Gates of Alexander
[14] http://islam101.net/real-tales-topmenu-39/53-real-tales/257-zul-qarnain.html

retrace the footsteps of *"Zul-Qarnain"* to verify the barrier he built to regulate Caucasus region savages seeing that it was aforementioned in Quranic history.

> *"In the year 643 AD Muslims' conquered Darband (named later 'Bab al-Abwab) in Dagestan Caucasus.* **Caliph Umar sent a group of Muslims to find and examine the barrier (wall) erected by Zul-Qarnain as described in Surah 18** *Al-Kahf of the Glorious Qur'aan. The wall was set up to prevent Yajooj wa Majooj (Gog and Magog) from their mischief and destruction. Upon receiving their report,* **Caliph Umar concluded that the wall was located in Darband.** *Hafiz Ibn Khatir mentions that Zul-Qarnain was a pious king, who lived during the time of Prophet Ibraheem and he performed the Tawaf of Ka'bah with Prophet Abraham (Ibraheem) when he built it.* **Dagestan is next to Chechnya (both are Muslim states) located in Caucasus, which is a region of southeast European U.S.S.R. between the Black and Caspian seas...*"*[15]

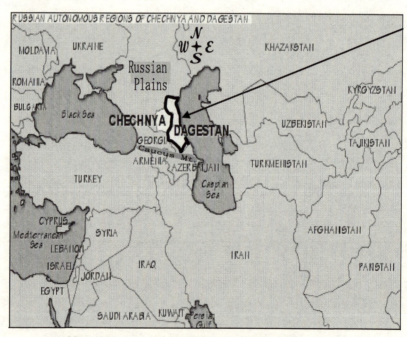

Map points out location of Dagstan (Darband)

---

[15] http://www.islam-is-the-only-solution.com/gmz.htm

White People

Quranic History 18:94-100

18:94 They said: O Dhu'l-Qarneyn! Lo! Gog and Magog are spoiling the land. So may we pay thee tribute on condition that thou set a barrier between us and them?
18:95 He said: That wherein my Lord hath established me is better (than your tribute). Do but help me with strength (of men), I will set between you and them a bank.
18:96 Give me pieces of iron - till, when he had leveled up (the gap) between the cliffs, he said: Blow! - till, when he had made it a fire, he said: Bring me molten copper to pour thereon.
18:97 And (Gog and Magog) were not able to surmount, nor could they pierce (it).
18:98 He said: This is a mercy from my Lord; but when the promise of my Lord cometh to pass, He will lay it low, for the promise of my Lord is true.
18:99 And on that day we shall let some of them surge against others, and the Trumpet will be blown. Then We shall gather them together in one gathering.
18:100 On that day we shall present hell to the disbelievers , plain to view,

Of course, by the time Arab Muslims set foot in Dagestan in 643 AD to verify the barrier (military fortress) established by *"the Zul-Qarnain factor"*, the once savage tribes of the Caucus Mountains had already produced ruling elites of religious leadership of Western Rome and established a religious concept extracted from Jewish PSEUDEPIGRAPHY. Except, in this case, Western Roman Church fathers went too far in corrupting scriptural content.

That is: *The Father, The Son and Holy Ghost*—notion solidified in 381 AD under the Nicene-Constantinopolitan Creed. Thus the Quran 18:15 read, *"Here are our people setting up gods beside Him. If only they could provide any proof to support their stand!* **Who is more evil than the one who fabricates lies and attributes them to GOD?'...** "

And so, it was the recessive (aa) gene race of people that religiously advertised *"in the name of The Father, The Son and Holy Ghost"* to unite Europe's pagan Scythian tribes. In this manner, their religion was more flexible than ancient monotheism. Afterward, Europe set out to completely overthrow the monotheistic biblical world of the aboriginal Black nations of the earth with lies, fairytales and holy wars.

"Say: *Shall We* [نَحْنُ nahnu] *inform you who will be the greatest losers by their works?"* (Quran 18:103)

FOUR
Black Man Of Ancient Europe

Certain members of ancient Scythians were once lead by certain ancient black tribes that provided for them 6,000 years ago. Some historians espouse certain ancient Scythians were mixed with Turkic blood. That is because they were mongrelizing and worshiping with blacks outside of the Caucus Mountain palisade while their other brethren were exiled into the Caucus Mountain palisade without any worthwhile worship (Selah). After 2,000 years without Selah, they became absolutely savage. So unlike their completely recessive blue-eyed, blood and red hair recalcitrant brethren, certain *Turkic* Scythians were Semitic by names sake, yet recessive too. All in all, pale skin people derived from the black (*AA*) gene pool into a recessive (*aa*) gene pool.

The wife of Messenger Elijah Muhammad, Mother Tynetta Muhammad, explains:

> "*A part of their race escaped* [eviction out of the Holy Land—Biblical Garden of Eden] *by hiding out in some of the homes of the Original People in Arabia* **and ultimately made their way into the hills of what we call Central Asia or Eurasia and lived among the Original People in those parts of our planet**.
>
> "*They did not go into the caves of Western Europe and took on the characteristics of the tribes living in that area of our planet.* **They were protected by the [Black] tribes in that entire area all the way into the Caucasus Mountains in Russia where they co-mingled with the people there and are recognized in the history as the Scythians and other Nomadic Tribes that lived around the Black Sea and the Caspian Sea.**
>
> "**Among the two branches of the Caucasian Race, the Jews who followed and strictly obeyed Moses Divine Law, were able to get out of their condition faster than the other members of their race.**" [June 9, 2009 Final Call Newspaper]

From the above explanation, there was once a group of "whites" that did not live among beast in caves because they were protected by black tribes of Central Asia (Armenia)—the Catal Huyuk culture or possibly the Grimaldi[16] before walking them into the Russian plains, Western Siberia and Ural Mountains. But as for those "whites" whom did go into the Caucus Iberie palisade, Mossa (Moses) had to first civilize them before they were able to enter into the cities south of the Caucasus Mountains, *Holy Quran 18:19.*

The final point to this particular matter surrounds the presence of an ancient Egyptian (Khem) colony discovered in the West Caucus Europe. In fact, this element of *"the Zul-Qarnain factor"* can be acknowledged even before the presence of King Cyrus and Darius arrived in Dagestan—East Caucus Europe. According the first Greek researcher and historian, Herodotus:

> *"It appears,"* says he, in his book *"Euterpe,"* *"that the inhabitants of* **Colchis sprang from Egypt**. *I judge so from my own observations rather than from hearsay; for I found that, at Colchis, the ancient Egyptians were more frequently recalled to my mind than the ancient customs of Colchis were when I was in Egypt.*

Map of Ancient countries of Caucasus: Armenia, Iberia

"These inhabitants of the shores of the Euxine Sea (Black Sea) stated themselves to be a colony founded by Sesostris (12th Dynasty Egyptian Ruler). As for myself, I

---

[16] Many thousands of years before the rise of the current pale tribes of Europe, an Afrocoid people known as the Grimaldi people, established the Aurignacian cultures. These people were anatomically modern human beings of the West African typology. They brought the first indications of cultural thoughts and rites into Europe. **[Source: http://jrmoore1958.tripod.com/grimaldi.html]**

*should think this probable, not merely because **they are dark and woolly-haired, but because the inhabitants of Colchis, Egypt, and Ethiopia are the only people in the world who, from time immemorial, have practised circumcision**; for the Phœnicians, and the people of Palestine, confess that they adopted the practice from the Egyptians. The Syrians, who at present inhabit the banks of Thermodon (N.E. Turkey), acknowledge that it is, comparatively, but recently that they have conformed to it. It is principally from this usage that they are considered of Egyptian origin."* [17]

It should be further stressed here, before Sesostris (Senusret)—12th Dynasty Egyptian ruler, before King Cyrus and king Darius, the Naqada culture of predynastic Egypt had prepared and sent Mossa (Musa) to the Caucus Mountains in 4000 BC with a host. Nevertheless, it appears from Greek historian observations, Colchis (West Caucus Europe) was a black civilization—the prime *"Zul-Qarnain factor"*, and continuum of the Selah of Musa and his host.

Sesostris

In addition, it was the Naqada culture where archeologist found white ivory figures with blue eyes. These figurines were non-Africoid and represented that predynastic Egyptian Priest knew about the pale skin, blue eyed race of men and women as the Holy Quran 18:21 revealed, *"We caused them to be discovered, to let everyone know that GOD's promise is true, and to remove all doubt concerning the end of the world."*

---

[17] http://www.cwo.com/~lucumi/georgia.html

Mossa (Moses or Musa) was educated at what once existed as *"the Ancient Egyptian Mystery School of Anu"*. He visited or was sent to the Caucus Mountains and cliffs to civilize whomsoever would bow down to cultic duties and temple hierarchy by his command. He was the first messenger of God to have accosted Caucasians after they'd spent 2,000 years outside of the civilized biblical world. Before Musa was sent, however, Caucasians were identified as "Set The Destroyer" according to ancient Egyptian theology.

"The earliest known representation of Set comes from a tomb dating to the Naqada I phase of the Predynastic Period (circa 4000 BC–3500 BC), and the Set-animal is even found on a mace-head of the Scorpion King, a Protodynastic ruler.

"Was ("power") scepters represent the Set-animal. Was scepters were carried by gods, pharaohs, and priests, as a symbol of power, and in later use, control over the force of chaos (Set). The head and forked tail of the Set-animal are clearly present. Was scepters are often depicted in paintings, drawings, and carvings of gods, and remnants of real Was scepters have been found constructed of faience or wood."[18]

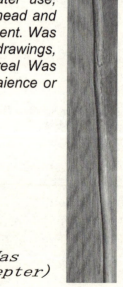

Was (Scepter)

---

[18] http://en.wikipedia.org/wiki/Was

Could **Set** have represented Europe's ancient Os**set**ia tribe, the most recalcitrant and belligerent tribe of the palisades of the Caucus Mountains? Whatever the case may be, it took about 80 years before Musa's earliest followers began entering the holy cities of the ancient southern hemisphere. Then, by waves, others made their way into Bactria, India while other waves attempted to enter Far East Asia, but the Great Wall of China was built to keep them out.

Map 4

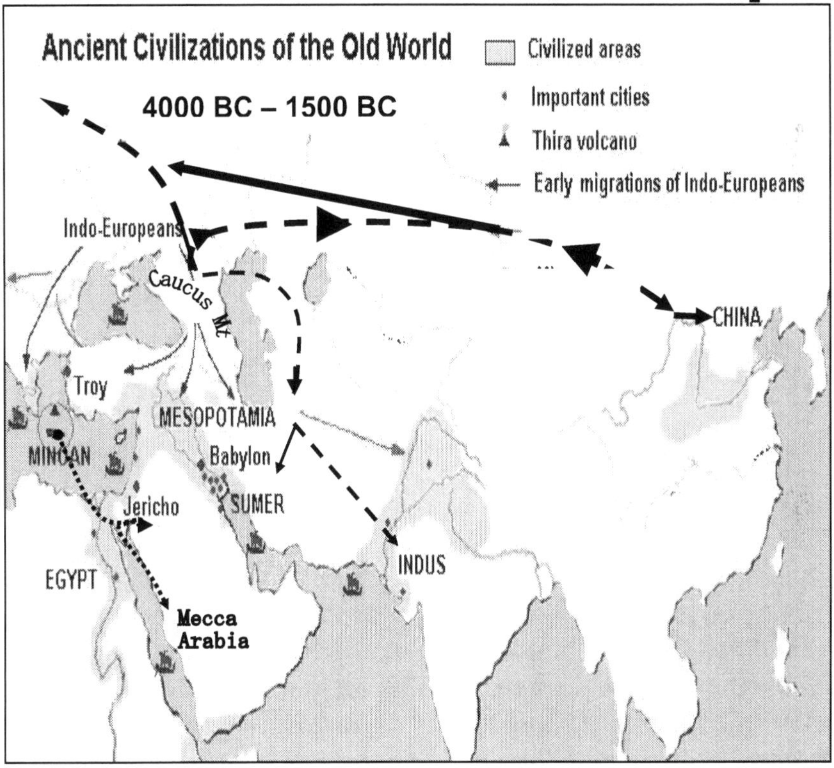

Ancient Civilizations of the Old World
4000 BC – 1500 BC
- Civilized areas
- Important cities
- Thira volcano
- Early migrations of Indo-Europeans

Indo-Europeans, Caucus Mt, Troy, MINOAN, MESOPOTAMIA, Babylon, Jericho, SUMER, EGYPT, Mecca Arabia, INDUS, CHINA

Map 4 above demonstrates their early movements out of the Caucus Mountains. The more rebellious Caucasians who were opposed to monotheism migrated down into the European continent, Germany, the Mediterranean, Northern Europe and the British Isles over the centuries. Based upon historical reports, the Ossetia, later known as Alani, may have been some of the last Caucasians to leave the Caucus Mountains. Allah knows best.

*"There are, perhaps, hundreds of miscellaneous books, scientific papers and articles written in different countries of the world about the **Ossetians... living mainly in the central part of the Caucasus mountain range**. What compelled so much of the world leading historians,' linguists' and archeologists' attention to **this small ancient nation, lost in the mountain country of the Caucasus**?*

*"To understand who the modern **Ossetians are**, one should go back in time for thousands of years, to the period when, as it is now believed, some part of those who made up the **Indo-European race separated from the rest of their tribesmen and headed for the Middle Asia and Northern Iran**. Part of this people, conspicuous for its belligerence and recalcitrance, in the course of time...**The mixing of the Scythians with the ancient Cobanians provided an important platform for the formation of the Ossetian people**.*

*"**The Ossetians are a clearly Indo-European people; quite a few of them have fair or chestnut hair, grey or blue eyes**. The same features, as it is known, were inherent in many Sarmatians."*[19]

Map 5 on the next page demonstrates major Scythian Alan (Alani) migrations in the 4th–5th centuries. During this time, Persia's monotheistic rule swayed power in central Asia replacing Southern Mediterranean Assyria's version of power, rulership and revised religious interpretation.

In any event, Musa' converts are the *"people of the book."* They made their initial outward movements into central Asia, Asia Minor and elsewhere. Their acrimonious impact would have occurred between 4000 – 3100 BC. From this age, warfare in the biblical region exacerbated.

---

[19] http://www.southosetia.euro.ru/en_whoos.html

Map 5

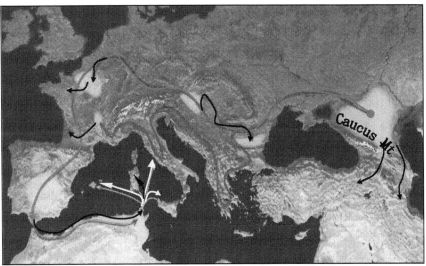

From the Caucus Mountains and Russian plains, from Siberia and Ural Mountains they invaded the holy cities of the southern hemisphere. Before that, 6,000 years ago, from the Aegean Sea, they invaded the holy city Mecca, according to the teachings of the Honorable Elijah Muhammad. (See Appendix 1, pg. 100, Failure of the Turks) Consequently felicity slowly declined throughout the holy precincts and cities of ancient world centers of learning.

Black People

FIVE
Mediterranean Caucasoid

Some Anthropologist believe "Mediterranean" means "Southern Caucasoid." Such ethnic stock, according the teachings of the Nation of Islam, is the geographical region from where the recessive (*aa*) gene race was born 6,000 years ago as a result of Yacub—the biblical Jacob. This is why the Holy Quran 15:26-31 reads, "26. *Verily We* [نَحْنُ *nahnu*] *created man of potter's clay of black mud altered. 27. And the jinn did We* [نَحْنُ *nahnu*] *create aforetime of essential fire. 28. And (remember) when thy Lord said unto the angels: Lo! I am creating a mortal out of potter's clay of black mud altered, 29. So, when I have made him and have breathed into him of My Spirt, do ye humble yourselves unto him 30. So the angels fell prostrate, all of them together. 31. Except, Iblis. He refused to prostrate.*" In one degree, not all of the ancients approved the new profound status that the Caucasian civilization was going to fulfill according to Allah (God's) decree. Therefore, conflicts occurred within the nucleus or inner circle of the Scientists of Islam. The Holy Quran 2:30-33; 40-42; 47-48 symbolically mentions this dispute. It mystically speaks of how one refused to bow down to Allah's (God's) temporary vicegerent because "he" knew who ruled first on the earth.

> "*30. Behold, thy Lord said to the angels: 'I will create a vicegerent on earth.' They said: 'Wilt Thou place therein one who will make mischief therein and shed blood?*- whilst we do celebrate Thy praises and glorify Thy holy (name)?' He said: 'I know what ye know not.' 31. And He taught Adam the nature of all things; then He placed them before the angels, and said: 'Tell me the nature of these if ye are right.' 32. They said: 'Glory to Thee, of knowledge We have none, save what Thou Hast taught us: In truth it is Thou Who art perfect in knowledge and wisdom.' 33...* **And behold, We said to the angels: 'Bow down to Adam' and they bowed down.**

Not so Iblis: he refused and was haughty: *He was of those who reject Faith...* **40**. *O Children of Israel! call to mind the (special) favour, which I bestowed upon you, and fulfill your covenant with Me as I fulfill My Covenant with you, and fear none but Me. 41.* ***And believe in what I reveal, confirming the revelation which is with you****, and be not the first to reject Faith therein, nor sell My Signs for a small price; and fear Me, and Me alone. 42.* ***And cover not Truth with falsehood, nor conceal the Truth when ye know*** *(what it is)... 47.* ***Children of Israel! call to mind the (special) favour which I bestowed upon you, and that I preferred you to all others (for My Message)****. 48. Then guard yourselves against a day when one soul shall not avail another nor shall intercession be accepted for her, nor shall compensation be taken from her, nor shall anyone be helped (from outside)."*

That is: the white race was chosen to govern the original nations of the earth for 6,000 years. All did not agree. Until this day, millions of aboriginal members of the African continent and India yet resist the rule of western capitalism—the financial apparatus by which Caucasoid rule dominates the nations of the earth.

October 13, 1972 {Muhammad Speaks Newspaper} the Honorable Elijah Muhammad revealed, **"We are four thousand years from Moses; and Moses was two thousand years after the creation of the Caucasian race, or two thousand years after the fathers of the Caucasian or white race of Europe. This makes six thousand years from the time of the birth or grafting of the Caucasian race. In four thousand years of the white man's rule they have practiced and exercised their power and authority over us as was divinely given to them..."** Whether or not all of the ancient religious scientists and rulers accepted Allah's decree regarding the future of the Caucasoid was immaterial because the end of "white" rule was also foretold. Calculatingly, the history of America, Great Britain, England, Belgium, Spain, Portugal, France, Italy and modern day Israel represents the end point or final accomplishment of the *"people of the book"* whom collectively was given 6,000 years to rule over the soul of the Black nation. Therefore

White People

Quran 18:7-13 testified, "9. **Or dost thou reflect that the Companions of the Cave and of the Inscription were wonders among Our Sign?** 10. Behold, the youths betook themselves to the Cave: they said, "Our Lord! bestow on us Mercy from Thyself, and dispose of our affair for us in the right way!" 11. **Then We draw (a veil) over their ears, for a number of years, in the Cave, (so that they heard not):** 12. **Then We roused them, in order to test which of the two parties was best at calculating the term of years they had tarried!** 13. We relate to thee their story in truth: they were youths who believed in their Lord, and **We advanced them in guidance:**"

The guidance given to the white race did not make them think independent of the original nations in terms of building material. Everything America and Europe has used to build its world government is only borrowed material from all previous ancient civilizations.

Western Semitic People In Central Asia and Musasir

Around 4500 BC a group of Southern Caucasoid who were later identified as Assyrians made their way from the Mediterranean into Central Asia. This meant the end of the Blackman's power to keep them in their boundaries of Europe. This brought them out of the caves putting them on the road to the conquest of Asia, (Black, Brown, Red and Yellow man.)[20]

After living among the aboriginal black nations of Mesopotamia/Sumer/Elam/Assur, an Assyrian Caucasoid government developed around 2500 BC wherein they had built three major cities in central Asia...[**For the future of the white race**], it is in Assyria where [**their version**] of the mythological foundation of the old and new testament is found. In one gist, the Assyrian concepts fulfilled a lesser degree about those whom the Quran labels *"people of the book."* It is here [**Assyria's Babylon**] that the history of the

---
[20] www.muhammadspeaks.com/Nimrod.html

flood originates, 2,000 years before the Old Testament is [re]written. It is here that the first Epic of Gilgamesh,[21] the story of wild man who is tamed from living a savage beast life before allowed to live among civilized people, is [re]written. It is here that civilization itself is developed and handed down to future generations. It is here where the first steps in the cultural unification of the Middle East are taken by bringing under Assyrian rule the diverse groups in the area, from Iran to Egypt, breaking down ethnic and national barriers and preparing the way for the cultural unification which facilitated the subsequent spread of Hellenism, Judaism, Christianity and Islam. Hence, the "first golden age of Assyrian history" commences [**in Assyria's subordination of ancient central Asian socio-economic and religious order**].

Map 6

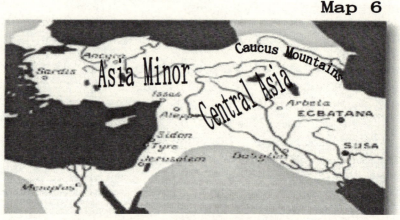

Map of Assyrian empire 2500 BC – 612 BC

BC 745-727, the Assyrian empire would extend its rule over a vast area, from Egypt up to Cyprus to the west, through Anatolia, to the Caspian in the east as shown in Map 6. This period would see 1800 years of Caucasoid Assyrian hegemony over Mesopotamia (Assur), beginning with

[source www.jstor.org/pss/4299853]

Sargon of Akkad in 2371 B.C. and ending with the tragic fall of Nineveh in 612 B.C.[22]

When the Mediterranean Caucasoid Assyrian reign concluded, Achaemenid Persians were being prepared to take the reigns over the ancient biblical regions. They were to police what *Southern Caucasoid* Assyrians had greatly disrupted during their 1800 year reign in central Asia and Asia Minor. For the *people of the book* were not yet advanced with enough guidance from Allah to uphold Yacub's (Jacob) world together until its appointed term.

> *"IN OUR 25-thousand-year cycle of making history for our Nation, there was a vacuum of 6,000 years. This Yakub, the father of the white man, was aware of. Therefore, he put his made-man in the vacuum to rule. This vacuum extended from the 9,000th year to the 15,000th year of our calendar history, so God (in the Person of Master Fard Muhammad) to whom praises are due forever, taught me. His making the made-man unalike to attract alike was a perfect job. He foresaw the end of the unalike made-man, and was perfect in knowledge that this type man could rule alike (the original man). Therefore, Mr. Yakub's idea became a fruitful one. He would make a man an enemy to his original self and kind, (Yakub was an original man.) This made-man's wisdom had no permanence and would be limited to the coming of an alike person to take over his way of rule...*
>
> *"SO OUR fathers of 6,000 years ago (the original Black man of Arabia) saw this unalike person emerging from the Island of the Aegean Sea and were attracted by this people----so much so that they began to take them as friends and even to marry them and hide them away in their homes. They had been attracted by an unalike person. They had never seen a white human being before. He was not made in Arabia but he was made out of Arabia on an Island in the sea. He was not allowed to be made in the Holy Land. As the Bible teaches us, when Yakub's knowledge or idea of making the made-man was discovered*

---

[22] www.aina.org/aol/peter/brief.htm#Racial

they cast him and those who believed with him out (you will find this in Genesis) where it reads: "Drive him out lest he put his hand on the tree of life and live forever."[23]

When the Muslim book of scripture, Holy Quran, mystically reveals how Caucasian people once upon a time dwelled in caves, it was actually uncovering the Jewish Mosaic calendars lost 2,000 years. These years were taken from the *people of the book* for rebelling against Allah's way of life in paradise 6,000 years ago.

Homeland of Early Civilized Whites

According to THE EARLY HISTORY OF INDO-EUROPEAN LANGUAGES by Thomas V. Gamkrelidze and V. V. Ivanov, *"The early investigators placed the homeland in Europe and posited migratory paths by which the daughter languages evolved into clearly defined Eastern or Western branches. Our work indicates that the proto-language originated more than 6,000 years ago in eastern Anatolia and that some daughter languages must have differentiated in the course of migrations that took them first to the East and later to the West.*

"The landscape described by the proto-language as now resolved must lie somewhere in the crescent that curves around the southern shores of the Black Sea, south from the Balkan peninsula, east across ancient Anatolia (today the non-European territories of Turkey) and north to the Caucasus Mountains. Here the agricultural revolution created the food surplus that impelled the Indo-Europeans to found villages and city-states from which, about 6,000 years ago, they began their migrations over the Eurasian continent and into history. Some of the migrants invaded Anatolia from the East around 2000 B.C. and established the Hittite kingdom, which held all of Anatolia in its power by 1400 B.C." [Source: Scientific American, March 1990, P.110]

---

[23] www.muhammadspeaks.com/Unalikeattracts4-5-1968.html

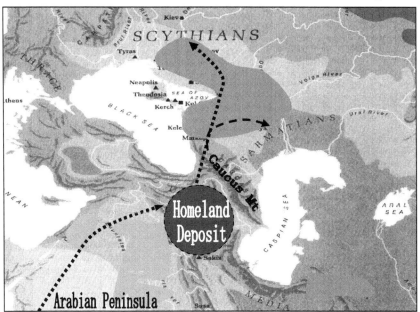

Map 7

Map 7 above outlines the first *"Indo-European"* who was moved out of the Arabian Peninsula to central Asia by blacks and then into the Russian plains, which gives weight to Mother Tynetta Muhammad's remarks about *Scythian* migrations. Did some of these Scythian tribes later become also known as Iranians and Khazars? And what gives with the city of Musasir located within the vicinity Europe's posited homeland, the Central-Asian steppe. Why did Assyrians begin their civilization in central Asia or Mesopotamia (Sumer) in 2500 BC?

As scholars deduce, the teachings of the Honorable Elijah Muhammad and the Nation of Islam brought clarity to what was once hidden for 6,000 years about the making of the Caucasian race or Yacub's grafted devil—the adversaries of the One God—monotheism and its rule of law. More on this subject in chapter 7.

Iran

The Central-Asian steppe has been the home of Scythian nomad tribes for centuries. Being nomads, they roamed across the plains, raiding the urbanized cities to the north, south, east and west. The first to describe the life style of these tribes was a Greek researcher, Herodotus, who lived in the fifth century BCE. Although he concentrates on the tribes living in modern Ukraine, which he calls Scythians, we may extrapolate his description to people in Kazakhstan, Turkmenistan, Uzbekistan, Tajikistan, Kyrgyzstan and possibly Mongolia, even though Herodotus usually calls these eastern nomads 'Sacae'.

In fact, just as the Scythians and the Sacae shared the same life style, they had the same name: in their own language, which belonged to the Indo-Iranian family, they called themselves *Skudat* ('archers'). The oldest group we know of is usually called Indo-Iranian. (The old name 'Aryan' is no longer used.)... In the sixth, fifth and fourth centuries BCE, the Persians discerned several nomad tribes on the Central-Asian steppe...they called them Sakâ. We know the names of these tribes from Persian royal inscriptions and can add information from Herodotus and other Greek authors.[24]

In more ways then one, Persians are related to Scythians and Scythians are related to Persians. The power was demonstrated twice with this particular race, first with Zoroastrianism and second with Islam. But it was Zoroastrianism, a monotheistic concept, in which the Achaemenid Persian Empire employed to battle against what Caucasoid Assyrians, I reiterate, disrupted in central Asia. After the Achaemenid Persians exhausted their energy, then came the Parthian Scythian Persians. This race migrated from Dahae to Bactria and then into what is now called Iran

---

[24] http://www.iranchamber.com/history/articles/scythians_sacae.php

where they fought off Roman invaders in central Asia, Mesopotamia. (See map 8 and 9)

> "The Parthians were a subgroup of the nomadic steppe culture known to us as the Scythians. Tradition has it that they conquered the region known in the ancient period as Parthia (now part of Iran) during 400 BC under <u>Arsaces I</u>.

Coinage Image of Arsaces I

> "Arsaces was the leader of a small nomadic group known as the Parni which were a part of the Dahae confederation of tribes centered around the eastern Caspian in present-day Turkistan".[25]

---

[25] americanhistory.si.edu/collections/numismatics/parthia/frames/phisfm.htm

In 150 BC Mesopotamia was under the control of the Parthian Persians. Mesopotamia became a battle ground between the Romans and Parthians, with parts of Mesopotamia (particularly Assyria) coming under periodic Roman control. In 226 AD it fell to the Sassanid Persians, and remained under Persian rule until the 7th century AD during the Arab Islamic conquest of the Sassanid Persian Empire (mixture of Achaemenid and Parthian races).

On page 54 you'll see comparisons between ancient Scythian (Saka) territories with their modern day names and territories shown on map 8 and map 9.

Most Scythians remained rather barbaric, pagan and polytheistic. But the Scythians under Zoroastrian-monotheism from 500 BC to the present monotheism-Islam have remained firm against Satan to the best of their ability considering one of the world's ancient civilizations, Mesopotamia (modern day Iraq), was at last totally destroyed in 2001 by the *people of the book*.

"[19]*Babylon* **[Mesopotamia, Iraq]**, *the jewel of kingdoms, the glory of the Babylonians' pride, will be overthrown by God like Sodom and Gomorrah.* [20]*She will never be inhabited or lived in through all generations; no Arab will pitch his tent there, no shepherd will rest his flocks there.* [21]*But desert creatures will lie there, jackals* **[dogs]** *will fill her houses; there the owls will dwell, and there the wild goats will leap about.* [22]*Hyenas will howl in her strongholds, jackals in her luxurious palaces. Her time is at hand, and her days will not be prolonged.*" (Isaiah 13:19-22)

Isaiah's passage, in the short term, was brought into play by the people of the book to justify the destruction of Mesopotamia (Iraq) under the guise of WMD (Weapons of Mass Destruction). But in the long term, prior to Jewish-Christian psuedopigraphic, the destruction of Babylon pointed to America—the kingdom where God Himself is going to Judge like Sodom and Gomorrah.

White People

"In this time, in which we are now living, there is no respect for dignity -- the President leaving the country to travel afar, to meet with rulers of foreign countries to discuss the strange things that are happening, and the strange things that will happen between the nations. The beautiful and rich country of America, to which many people of Europe and Asia migrated, seeking refuge -- in this country, as the prophecy is now coming into fulfillment...("...in that day and time everyone will begin to go away from America, instead of coming to America!")

"As the Revelation (Bible) teaches us of the prophecy that "they will stand afar off and see the fire of her (America's) burning and for fear of it they will lift up their hands and their voices. They will lament for her!" America's trade is cut off and all of her delicious and delicate things that she used to have in trade -- it is all gone! In one hour (one day) it came to pass, here in the Western Hemisphere!

"The most wicked people who ever lived on the earth is in the Western Hemisphere, as the Bible teaches us that God said, that to Him this is like Sodom and Gomorrah. He (Allah) (God) did say that 'The wickedness of the day of Noah and his people, and Lot and his people, (the Sodomites) was no more than child's play compared to the wickedness of today, for they are highly educated -- they are scientists at making wickedness for themselves.' Day and night, up and down the streets, people are killing, murdering each other! The radio and the television announce to the public that murdering and killings are taking place continually.[26]

---

[26] www.muhammadspeaks.com/FOA60.html

Black People

Map 8

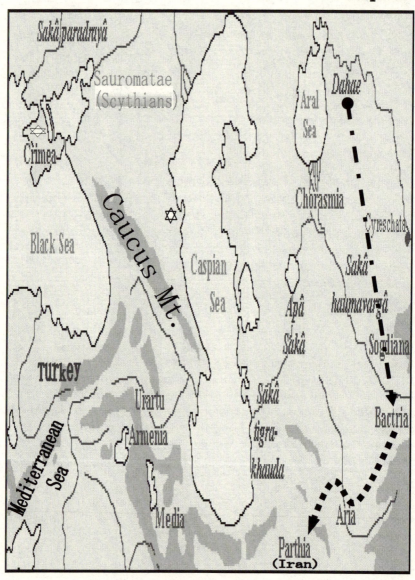

Map 9

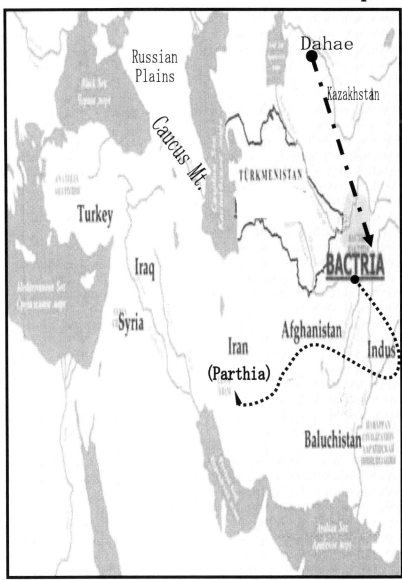

Some historians contend Dravidians of ancient Black India (Indus Valley) transmitted "Zoroastrianism" to the

Scythian prophet, Zarathushtra, in the form of ancient holy writings. Historians maintain he was born in 650 BC.

"Bactria was the homeland of Aryan tribes who moved south-west into Iran and into North-Western India around 2500-2000 BC. [Review maps on pages 54-55]

"Later it became the north province of the Persian Empire in Central Asia. It was in these regions, where the fertile soil of the mountainous country is surrounded by the Turanian desert, that the prophet Zarathushtra (Zoroaster) was said to have been born and gained his first adherents. Avestan, the language of the oldest portions of the Zoroastrian Avesta, was once called "old-iranic" which is related to Sanskrit.

"Today some scholars believe the Avestan-Language was the western dialect of the Sanskrit because both languages are the oldest Indo-Iranian language of Aryans we know. With the time the Avestan-Language became developed by own western style.

"Bactria was bounded on the south by the ancient region of Gandhara. The Bactrian language is an Iranian language of the Indo-Iranian sub-family of the Indo-European family.[27]

In conclusion, Persian leaders have continued their observation of the One God monotheistic concept, to the best of their ability. In as much as Iranian Scythians were able to make the transition from Zoroasterism into Islam as it was foretold according to the ancient Zoroaster holy book – The Vesta Holy text, she has maintained an unbroken chain of governance for thousands of years.

---

[27] http://encyclopedia.stateuniversity.com/pages/2246/Bactria.html

"The Zoroastrian holy scriptures has changed over time. The Gathas were the original revelation, which Zoroaster delivered to his people. Only 5 books have survived. The scripture was first written in Gathic; a dead language which is reserved for few scholars only. Later Priests would add to the Gathas, in the Avestan language, to make up the rest of the Zoroastrian holy book, now known as the Avesta (or Zend Avesta). This book was translated by the conquering Sassanid's into the Pahlavi tongue. What survives today is estimated to be only a quarter of the original 21 books of the Avesta.

"The excerpt displayed here is from a portion of the Avesta known as the Dadistan. The prophecy specifically contained in Sasan 1, verses 54-61:

"When such deeds the Persians will commit, a man from among the Arabs will be born, from among the followers of whom, crown and throne, and kingdom and religion of the Persians all shall be overthrown and dissolute. And the arrogant people shall be subjugated. They will see instead of the house of idols and the temple of fire, the house of worship of Abraham without any idols in it; the Qibla. And they will be a mercy for the worlds and then they will capture places of the temples of fire, Madain or Ctesiphon, and of the surrounding places of eminence and sanctity, and their religious leader will be an eloquent man and his message or what he will say will be well connected.[28]

By AD 900's and 1000's, Islam became the dominant religion in Persia (modern day Iran). Subsequently, their conversion to Islam brought profound changes to their life and culture.

---

[28] http://www.islamicweb.com/beliefs/comparative/other_scriptures.htm

SIX
Mountain Jews

Mountain Jews, Juvuro, Juhuro of the eastern Caucasus, mainly of Azerbaijan and Dagestan, are known as **Caucasus Jews, Caucasian Jews**, or more uncommonly **East Caucasian Jews**. In terms of ethnic origin, it is assumed that the Mountain Jews and Tats (Iranian Aryan Muslims) have inhabited Caucasia for a long time.

Mountain Jews

Mountain Jews distant forefathers once lived in southwest Persia, the southwestern part of present-day Iran. Having become largely assimilated, the predecessors of the Mountain Jews settled on the west coast of the Caspian Sea in the 5th--6th century and from that time on their history has been related to the mountains and the people of Dagestan. While elsewhere in the Jewish Diaspora it was forbidden to own and till land, the Jews of Central Asia, were farmers and gardeners, growing mainly grain.[29] *"So the LORD God banished him from the Garden of paradise to work the ground from which he had been taken". (Genesis 3:23)* Were these Mountain Jews descendants of those whom called upon Zul-Qarnain (as mentioned in Holy Quran 18:94) for protection from the more fierce Caucus palisade tribes, in times past, *"They said, "O Zul-Qarnain, Gog and Magog are corruptors of the earth. Can we pay you to create a barrier between us and them?"*

---

[29] www.eki.ee/books/redbook/mountain_jews.shtml

Around 500's BC, Persia's Achaemenid State religion was Zoroastrianism, which is monotheistic in concept. In view of this, from a prophetic angle, the Achaemenid Persian Empire (modern day Iran) was once positioned to aid the people of Musa (Mossa) by combating the forces of evil and darkness that was arising out of the Caucus Mountains and Europe in general. By this I mean Persia's role was to regulate the more savage "Scythians", who are also *"people of the book"*, but in their hearts rejected monotheism. So at some point in time, it appears the "Persian Empire" was deployed into the Caucus Mountains to prevent a premature war between eastern and western Europe's fierce tribes (Gog and Magog) from destroying the process of their own resurrection out of a chaotic state of barbarity to fulfill what was foretold by Allah's permission.

> *"19. **When we resurrected them**, they asked each other, 'How long have you been here?' 'We have been here one day or part of the day,' they answered. 'Your Lord knows best how long we stayed here, so let us **send one of us with this money to the city**. Let him fetch the cleanest food, and buy some for us. **Let him keep a low profile, and attract no attention. 20. 'If they discover you, they will stone you, or force you to revert to their religion, then you can never succeed.'"* (Quran 18:19-20)

Within this passage, we are able to see how Moses *(the mythological **Pkharmat**)* was rebirthing thought among Caucus Mountain tribes (what we now know was near Mount Kazbek). Verse 19 also reveals he taught them how to initially conduct themselves among civilized city folk of central Asia. It testifies, *"keep a low profile",* meaning use tricks and lies to avoid being discovered, which is a part of what Mossa had to teach. Otherwise, white authority would not have succeeded throughout central Asia and Asia Minor after 4,000 BC. Coincidentally, near eastern scholarship suggests Moses Egyptian name is spelled **Ptah-Mose**.[30] His

---

[30] www.jstor.org/pss/542944

duty and mission had a duel purpose. The three root letters, **p-h-m,** of his Egyptian name also mean to give and bestow cultic duties and temple hierarchy.[31]

In 1933, the founder of the Nation of Islam, Master Wallace Fard Muhammad, asked his Messenger and student, Elijah Muhammad to following question:

> "Why did we run Yacob and his made Devil from the Root of Civilization, over the hot desert, into the caves of West Asia, as they now call it - Europe? What is the meaning of Eu and Rope? How long ago? What did the Devil bring with him? What kind of life did he live? And how long before Mossa [Musa] came to teach the Devil of the forgotten Tricknollegy?"

Elijah Muhammad's answer:

> "Because they had started making trouble among the righteous people telling lies. They accused the righteous people causing them to fight and kill one another. Yacub was an original man and was the Father of the Devil. He taught the Devils to do this devilishment.
>
> "The Root of Civilization is in the Arabian Desert. We took from them everything except the language and made him walk every step of the way. It was twenty- two hundred miles. He went savage and lived in the caves of Europe. Eu means hillsides and Rope is the rope to bind in. It was six thousand nineteen years ago.
>
> "Mossa came two thousand years later and taught him how to live a respectful life, how to build a home for himself and some of the Tricknollegy that Yacub taught him, which was devilishment - telling lies, stealing any how to master the original man.
>
> "Mossa was a half-original, a prophet, which was predicted by the Twenty-Three Scientists in the year, One - fifteen thousand nineteen years ago today".[32]

---

[31] www.ieiop.com/pub/03freilich_03fe1c81.pdf

Zoroastrianism

Moses (Mossa) did not instruct his people to submit to black authority or their pantheon god religion, which attempted to explain the tree of life (mind or knowledge of God). Therefore, monotheistic Zoroastrianism was tailor-made for the *Achaemenid* Scythian Indo-Iranian or Persian Empire during the era when they regulated the biblical world to indirectly assist the people of Moses until around 330 AD.

Zoroastrianism is considered one of the world's first monotheistic religions. Its overtones were derived from Egypt's 18th Dynastic ruler, Akhenaten, around 1350 BC (800 years before Persia began ruling the Biblical lands). Except up till then Akhenaten's monotheistic theology was not even new because it was venerated from Egypt's older kingdom between BC 2686-2181 and beyond.

Considering the time and deviations that became apparent throughout the biblical world, prophet hood ended in 400 BC. Such an action also meant the time was approaching for Yacub's rebellious race to take the keys (power) out of the hands of the ancient Biblical rulers; namely, Sumerian, Elamite, Jebusite, Mesopotamian and others. (See images of ancient black rulers of ancient biblical world)

Sumer king   Jebusite (Jerusalem)   Elam (Iran) ruler

www.realhistorvww.com/world historv/ancient/Elam Iran 1.htm

---

[32] /www.thenationofislam.org/lostfoundlesson.html

Thus says the LORD, 'The products of Egypt and the merchandise of Cush [black nation] and the Sabeans [Tribe of Queen Sheba], men of stature, will come over to you and will be yours; they will walk behind you, they will come over in chains And will bow down to you; They will make supplication to you: 'Surely, God is with you, and there is none else, No other God.'" (Isaiah 45:14)

People of The Book's Pseudepigrapha

Jewish Michael E. Stone, a Professor of Armenian Studies and of Religious Studies at the Hebrew University of Jerusalem writes *"**The term Pseudepigrapha (Greek, "falsely attributed") was given to Jewish writings** of the same period, which were attributed to authors who did not actually write them. **This was widespread in Greco-Roman antiquity - in Jewish, Christian, and pagan circles alike. Books were attributed to pagan authors, and names drawn from the repertoire of biblical personalities, such as Adam, Noah, Enoch, Abraham, Moses, Elijah, Ezekiel, Baruch, and Jeremiah.** The Pseudepigrapha resemble the Apocrypha in general character, yet were not included in the Bible, Apocrypha, or rabbinic literature. **All the Apocrypha and most of the Pseudepigrapha are Jewish works (some contain Christianizing additions).** They provide essential evidence of Jewish literature and thought during the period between the end of biblical writing (400 BC)[33] and the beginning of substantial rabbinic literature in the latter part of the first century CE. They have aroused much scholarly interest, since they provide information about Judaism at the turn of the era between the Bible and the Mishna (Biblical Law and Oral Law), and help explain how Rabbinic Judaism and*

---

[33] *"O People of the Book! now hath come unto you, making (things) clear unto you, Our Messenger, **after the break in (the series of) Our Messengers**, lest ye should say: "There came unto us no bringer of glad tidings and no warner (from evil)"; but now hath come unto you a bringer of glad tidings and a warner (from evil). And Allah hath power over all things."* (Quran 5.19)

Christianity came into being." That's why the Quran 5:77 testifies: *"...O People of the Book! exceed not in your religion the bounds (of what is proper), trespassing beyond the truth, nor follow the vain desires of people who went wrong in times gone by, who misled many, and strayed (themselves) from the even Way."*

Europeans Jews Western Europe had become unpopular. Their way of life was exclusive with synagogue schools for boys only. They allowed no pagan endogamy, read from their own religious text with an exegesis wherein Jews were the center of God's attention.

Recall, however, Mediterranean Caucasoid Assyrians instituted the first form of pseudepigrapha in 2500 BC; hence, the saga continued by Babylonian Assyrian Jews of 400 BC. Such pseudepigrapha became a collection of early Jewish and some Jewish-Christian writings made manifest between 200 BC and AD 200. These writings eventually were transmitted in Western Rome, Eastern Rome, Ethiopian and Egyptian Coptic churches. The legendary war of words during Greco-Roman antiquity between Christians and Jews became so intense around 200 AD those Christian *pseudepigrapha* included (Revelation 3:9) "Behold, I will cause those of the synagogue of Satan, who say that they are Jews and are not, but lie--

Jewish pseudepigrapha were written in the languages of Latin, Greek, Syriac, Georgian, Armenian, Coptic and Ethiopic though originally composed in Hebrew or Aramaic. That is to say, recalcitrant Caucasoid religious scientists essentially played with the previous scriptures that were left by Major Prophets of Asia Minor, Central Asia and Arabia until 400 BC.

Bible is Deluted

In 1934, the Elijah Muhammad published in "The Final Call to Islam" on august 18:

> "The whole contents of the Bible that you have predict the return of us back to Islam and Asia, our home. But remember that the same devils who enslaved our forefathers and ourselves DILUTED THE TRUTH IN THE BIBLE when they translated it out of the Greek tongues into the English language. It was originally given to the Hebrews by the Ethiopians (Moslems). The Asiatic Moslems knew that they would have a lost brother somewhere on the Planet Earth. But the Holy Quran did not say where he would be. But they all believed that in the devils civilization was where their lost brother would be. So they gave this warning Book (Bible) to the Jews (devils) that perchance if the lost brother would see it and read and understand its contents he would rise from the death of ignorance……..

> "…when our enemies understood that the Book was for us they slew every one of the Translators of the Bible as it was then in its truest sense. They finally got a bunch of wicked translators and through them they took out some of the truth and added lies to some parts of it. And that part which they did publish was put in symbolic words. So obsure is the truth in the American Bible that it took no less than the Saviour of the Lost Brother of Asia to unfold its contents."

It was not until 610 – 632 AD with the birth of Prophet Mohammed Ibn Abdullah of Arabia that *monotheism* was [re]instituted by the revelation of the Holy Quran. Prophet Mohammed was the final seal of Prophet Hood. And, the book revealed to him; for the ancient biblical world, was the last one, until the coming of God Himself—the Divine Supreme Being also styled as A Saviour would write a New One for life of the *Hereafter* Satan's world is destroyed.

Map 10 is an ancient world-view showing where Major Prophets preached, were rejected and even murdered for revealing the truth. I provided black dots to give a general idea of prophet locals from 6,000 BC to 632 AD.

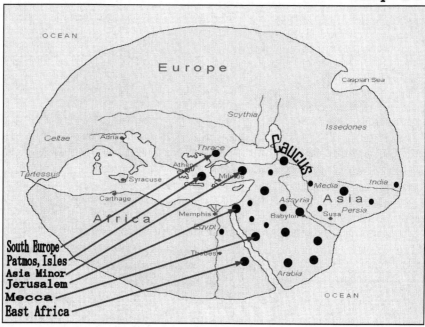

Map 10

Upon leaving the caves and cliffs of Europe, in 4000 BC, Caucasian scholars had exact access to Selah and the holy books only to dilute them at every opportunity. (See Appendix 2, List of Prophets Pg. 104)

Ironically, the ancient One God monotheistic theology; as well as pantheon god notions, originated with members of the Black nation. Subsequently, prophets were sent to aboriginal nations and Semite races too. Caucasians of West Asia were moreover, a recipient of previous divine scriptures after the fact because they were bound to the hills and caves 2,000 years of their 6,000 years of existence. Therefore, they were dubbed the *people of the book*—the lost tribe of Israel or Caucasian race whom "**P**tah-**M**ose" was sent to retrieve 4000 BC.

Recall, the Honorable Elijah Muhammad revealed that Moses (**P**tah-**M**ose) was *half Black and half white* (half original man) and his presence among Caucasians in Europe—West Asia was to, in part; teach them *"how to live a respectful life...and how to master the original man."* This guidance for a respectful life and dominion came in the form of religion as the Holy Quran 18:21 reveals: *"We [نَحْنُ nahnu] caused them to be discovered, to let everyone know that Allah's promise is true, and to remove all doubt concerning the end of the world. The people then disputed among themselves regarding them. Some said, "Let us build a building around them." Their Lord is the best knower about them. Those who prevailed said, "We will build a place of worship around them."*

The reason I accent the Arabic word *nahnu* [نَحْنُ] *(We)* in verse 21 is because within *nahnu*, is the name **anu**. To the same extent, the *Anu Priesthood* is identified with the pre-dynastic progenitors of ancient Egypt's (Kemet) dynasties and their systems of learning, including its prophetic writings. What they observed in the cosmological realm was a) interpreted, b) written in stone c) transferred to scrolls and d) spoken in words.

> *"This civilization called Egyptian in our period developed for a long time in its early cradle...This cycle of civilization, the longest in history, presumably lasted 10,000 years. This is a reasonable compromise between the long chronology (based on data provided by* **Manetho—the last student of the Ancient Egyptian Mystery School of Anu at Alexandria before it was invaded by Alexander the Great in 330 BCE-- which places the beginning at 17,000 BCE)** *and the short chronology [3,100 BCE] of the moderns - for the latter are obliged to admit that by 4,245 BCE the Egyptians had already invented the calendar (which necessarily requires the passages of thousands of years).*

> *"The common ancestor of the Annu settled along the Nile was Ani or An, a name determined by the word (khet) and which, dating from the earliest versions of the 'Book of the Dead' (4,100 BCE) onwards, is given to the god Osiris...*

The identity of the god An with Osiris has been demonstrated by Pleyte; we should indeed, recall that Osiris is also surnamed by the Anu: 'Osiris Ani'... **Are the Aunak tribes now inhabiting the upper Nile (in Ethiopia) related to the ancient Annu? Future research will provide the answer to this question.**

Modern Aunak

Ancient Anu Priest

"The leaders and staff of the Ancient Egyptian Mystery School of the ANU from TA-NETJER ("God's Land") were by definition priests who had attained spiritual deification and become 'human gods' called in the ancient documents of Egypt/Kemit as the aakhu-hammet or 'Sun People'. By 4,241 BC they had worked out the Sidereal Calendar and by 4,100 BCE they were using the PER-UM-HERU ("Book of Coming Forth by Day"). **The School of Anu trained amongst others Vizar Imhotep (2,650 BCE), Pharaoh Amenemhet III ("Memnon" 1,843 to 1,797 BCE), Pharaoh-Queen Hatshepsut (1,484-1,462 BCE), Pharaoh Thuthmoses III and IV, and his Prime Minister YU-SEFI or YU-SEP (Joseph of the Bible, 1,500-1,429 BCE). At the Temple of WA-SET built by Amenhotep III (1,391 BCE), students Pharaoh Akhenaton and Queen Nefertiti (1,350-1,340 BCE), Thales (600 BCE), Plato (400 BCE, studied 11 years), Socrates (15 years), Aristotle (11-13 years) Euclid (20 years), studied along with Pythagoras, Solon, Archimedes, Euripides, Herodotus and 80,000 other students."**

Akhenaton

"During the first half of the 18th Dynasty, Egyptian rulers began calling themselves "Thutmose" which means "reborn son of Thoth". Thoth was the mispronunciation of Dje-Hu-Ti or Ta-Hu-Ti (shortend to Ta-Hut, Thut, and finally Thoth).

> *Thoth, Thot, or Hermes as he was known to the Greeks is the last divine personage of the ancient pre-dynastic Anu....*
>
> **"To Thot [thought] we may attribute writing medicine, chemistry, law, rhetoric, the higher aspects of mathematics, astronomy and astrology, not to mention the early Egyptian understanding of the intricate dynamics of universal order.**
>
> *"Thoth or Thot was divine mind. He was known as the messenger of the gods... The word 'thought' is derived from this deity's name Thot.*
>
> *"Francis Barret said of Thoth, 'If God ever appeared in man, he appeared in him.' Legend holds that Thoth was the grand architect of the Great Pyramid aided by a high priest named RA or Ra Ta, and Isis, as counselor and advisor. This is said to have taken place in the year 10,490 BCE.* [34]

The above quote is only some of the great secrets that Caucasoid civilization works around the clock to keep hidden from the world at large. Nevertheless, not only is God a member of the Black nation, He and his angels are the (We) nahnu [نَحْنُ]) of the Holy Quran; yet alive and well. This circle of ancient Asiatic Scientists was preserved throughout the ages of time for the end times!

> *"...God is a Production made by the Action of Time... Their wisdom and work may live six thousand or twenty-five thousand years, but the actual individual may have died within a hundred or two hundred years, or the longest that we have a record of, around a thousand years. There is no God Living Who was here in the Creation of the Universe, but They produce Gods from Them and Their Wisdom lives in us."* [Elijah Muhammad, Chapter 19, Our Saviour Has Arrived]

Genesis 1:26 represents the beginning of white civilization—Adam, the recessive (aa) gene man. **"Then God said, "Let us make man in our image, in our likeness, and let them rule over the fish of the sea and the birds of the air, over the livestock, over all the earth, and over all the creatures that**

---

[34] http://www.rastafarispeaks.com/cgi-bin/forum/archive1/config.pl?read=55043

move along the ground." Moses (prophet Mossa) was prepared by the nahnu [نَحْنُ]) of the Holy Quran to resurrect them out of total darkness and ignorance as a sign of Allah's mercy in 4000 BC. This is why the Bible {Acts 7:22-23} testifies: *"**Moses was educated in all the wisdom of the Egyptians and was powerful in speech and action. 23. When Moses was forty years old, he decided to visit his fellow Israelites**".* In truth, Moses (Mossa) did not decide to visit his fellow Israelites—Caucasians. He was sent to them from Egypt's pre-dynastic Naqada culture to perform a duty. Old Caucus Mountain legends signify him under the name Pkharmat. (See Appendix 3, Pkharmat pg. 109)

Although the following Judeo-Christian pseudepigrapha narrative rewrote and retold how they would take dominion from the elder original nations, the truth of the matter was clarified by the teachings of the Honorable Elijah Muhammad and the Nation of Islam.

"Jacob later deceived his blind old father Isaac into pronouncing over him the blessings intended for the firstborn son, Esau.

*"**The Children of Israel** (the **Jew**ish tribes descended from Jacob, whose name was later changed to Israel,...*

*Jews, Hebrews, Children of Israel went to Egypt to escape a famine, but became enslaved there for 200 years. When Moses led them out of slavery, it was to reach their Promised Land. This was the land, which God had promised them, their inheritance. **God had told Moses to say to them, 'I will bring you to the land I swore to give to Abraham, to Isaac and to Jacob.' (Exodus 6:8)**...* [35]

According the Nation of Islam, these divinations were originally taught to Yacub's made race (white race) while they were still on the Aegean isles and/or Mediterranean area. Once they left the islands toward the Holy Land 6,000

---

[35] http://www.crossref-it.info/articles/26/Inheritance-and-heirs

years ago, upon entry they were received before they were expelled into the Caucasus palisade to live among beasts. After 2,000 years, Musa was sent. Then 2,000 thereafter Jesus was sent to the *people of the book*. However, after preaching in South Europe and Jerusalem their response to his words prompt him to realize how the people of Moses had made people like the children of hell.

*"Then **spake Jesus** to the multitude, and to his disciples, Saying 'The scribes and the Pharisees sit in Moses seat':...'Woe unto you, scribes and Pharisees, hypocrites! for ye compass sea and land to make one proselyte, and when he is made, ye make him twofold more the child of hell than yourselves.'" (Matthew 23:1-2:15)*

To the degree Jesus saw how the *"people of the book"* (Yacub's grafted race) had failed to carryout their religious obligation, to the degree monotheistic concepts were crushed, to the degree Jewish spiritual and political leadership surrendered to Greek Hellenism (religion of Assyria's Nimrod) Jesus of 2,000 years ago aborted his mission. He realized Yacub's grafted race had 2,000 more years to rule before God in Person and His army would be prepared to remove Yacub's creation from the seat of power and authority forever.

The book said Adam was given six days (6,000 years) to rule. For this reason, it was written in Divine scripture, **"Last of all, as though to one born at the wrong time, he appeared to me also." (1 Corinthians 15:8)** Christian scholars decode Corinthians 15:8 to mean Jesus was born ahead of his time. The linear calendar below confirms their point.

1 ----- 2 ----- 3 ----- 4 ---- 5 --- 6	= Days
Adam Musa Jesus	
4000 BC 2000 BC 1 AD	
2000 + 2000 + 2000	= 6,000 yrs.

The Honorable Elijah Muhammad and the Nation of Islam revealed, *"THOSE OF us who hope to see him [Jesus] come to life and guide us though the resurrection are gravely mistaking the scriptures and the history taught of Jesus. Let us face the truth and believe the truth and speak the truth. The Holy Qur'an makes him only a prophet. The Bible also, teaches us he was only a prophet. Other people have made us believe that he was God Himself and that he was not sent. --That he was incapable of dying -- but did die...that God will forgive Israel and that Israel will be reconciled to God as a people of righteousness. This is wrong. I am sure that if you study his history you will find that he did not say that he would die for Israel. Israel, by nature, was made wicked by their father, Yakub...*

"ONLY a few white people who because of their belief or faith in the truth of entire submission to the Will of God (Islam) have been promised by God, Himself, the salvation of a prolonged life through the resurrection and after the resurrection as a reward for their belief and their attempts to live the life of the Muslim. Yet, by nature, they are not one of the righteous. There are some here and there around us and in a country such as Europe who are trying to practice Islam. They will be rewarded for it. Their reward will be to live through the resurrection of us, the mentally dead, Lost and Found Members of our Nation.[36]

"And there are, certainly, among the people of the Scripture (Jews and Christians), those who believe in Allah and in that which has been revealed to you, and in that which has been revealed to them, humbling themselves before Allah. They do not sell the Verses of Allah for a little price, for them is a reward with their Lord. Surely, God is Swift in account". '(3:199)'

---

[36] www.muhammadspeaks.com/TrueHistoryJesus.html

SEVEN
Nimrod Ruins Moses' Civilization

King Darius

After the death of King Cyrus, king Darius the Great managed not only to hold together the *Achaemenid* Persian Empire from 522 to 486 BC but also extended its territory. I surmised earlier that Zul-Qarnain of the Holy Quran also represents a continuum of the ancient monotheistic governments of ancient Egypt's 12th century kings of 1950 BC. Therefore, Darius who further extended his troops to protect the descendants of the people whom Moses (Mossa) rose out of the caves of Europe represented mercy to the *people of the book*. But he had to also make war against the more savage tribes of that age to regulate central Asia's kingdoms.

Written on the tomb of King Darius, he leaves a testimony about how his God favored him to rule beyond Persia's immediate boarders.

"I am Darius the great king, king of kings, king of countries containing all kinds of men, king in this great earth far and wide, son of Hystaspes, an Achaemenid, a Persian, son of a Persian, an Aryan, having Aryan lineage.

"King Darius says: By the favor of Ahuramazda these are the countries which I seized outside of Persia; I ruled over them; they bore tribute to me; they did what was said to them by me; they held my law firmly; Media, Elam, Parthia, Aria, Bactria, Sogdia, Chorasmia, Drangiana, Arachosia, Sattagydia, Gandara, India, the haoma-drinking Scythians, the Scythians with pointed caps, Babylonia, Assyria, Arabia, Egypt, Armenia, Cappadocia, Lydia, the Greeks, the Scythians across the sea, Thrace, the sun hat-wearing

Greeks, the Libyans, the Nubians, the men of <u>Maka</u> and the <u>Carians</u>." [37]

Notice how Darius the Great proudly boosts about his Aryan (Scythian) blood. He was "half black and half white" Semitic. Political alliances was primary to fulfill certain prophecies and aims, therefore, inner racial marriages between black and white was in vogue among the ruling circles.

Map 11

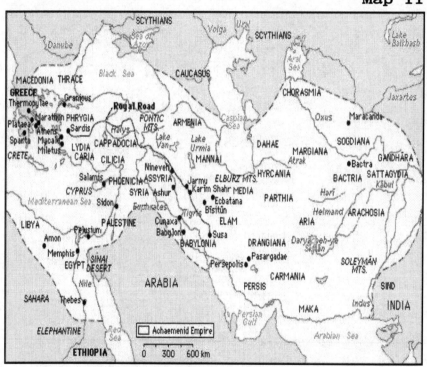

Map 11 shows how wide and vast king Darius and his generation advanced the *Achaemenid* Empire.

---

[37] http://www.livius.org/da-dd/darius/darius_i_t01.html#Upper

White People

According to a relief about king Darius, his rule and expansion demonstrated the power of Ahuramazda—God of Zoroastrianism—permitting him to conquer and maintain the known Biblical world.

> *"In Persian belief, Ahura Mazdah ("Lord Wisdom") was the supreme god who created the heavens and the Earth, and another son of Zurvan. Atar, his son, battled Azhi Dahaka, the great dragon of the sky, and bound it in chains on a high mountain. The dragon was, however, destined to escape and destroy a third of mankind at the final reckoning, before it was slain. Ahura Mazdah was the god of prophetic revelation, and bore both Ahriman and Ormazd. As leader of the Heavenly Host, the Amesha Spentas, he battles Ahriman and his followers to rid the world of evil, darkness and deceit.*[38]

The reign of Darius lasted thirty-five years and completed the work of his Achaemenid Persian Empire predecessors. It is apparent by the above quote that the ancient religious Scientists or priesthood understood the people of the "Mountains" represented an impending danger. They knew these "Mountain" people would no longer remain fixed to West Asia and would perpetuate mischief and bloodshed throughout the earth. Thus the great Zoroastrian prophecy pointed toward a war between God's people and the Devil's people at the end of the world.

The Winged Ones

Biblical Genesis 3:24 reads, *"So he sent the man out; and at the east of the garden of Eden **he put winged ones and a flaming sword turning every way** to keep the way to the tree of life."* This same verse is also written in these words, *"**And he cast out Adam; and placed before the paradise of pleasure Cherubims,** and a flaming sword, turning every way, **to keep the way of the tree of life.**"*

---

[38] http://www.pantheon.org/articles/a/ahura_mazda.html

Ancient Anatolia (Turkey) was the landmass where armed soldiers *(Cherubim or wing ones)* were placed to keep Yacub's Adamic race out of holy land (paradise). Verse 24 vaguely foretold about them being exiled into the Caucus Mountains under the command of General Munk Munk and his army of black Asiatics (*Cherubim or wing ones*) whom he had assigned to keep the Adamic race out the east (paradise) away from the tree of life i.e., knowledge of God.

In a much as Asia Minor—modern day Turkey represented the boundary separating the two people (Black and White) 6,000 years ago, around 1182 BC north-west Turkey was compromised thus enabling the blonds to settle Rome.

> *"According to Francis Owen in The Germanic People (1960), the people which settled Rome may have been immigrants from outside the Italian peninsula, possibly an off-shoot from the same group that would become Celtic or Germanic peoples. Traces of the founding population were apparently evident in the appearance of the aristocracy long into the time of the republic. According to Owens the evidence available from Roman literature, historical records and statuary and personal names shows that in physical appearance the Roman aristocracy differed from most of the population in the rest of the peninsula. The records describe a very large number of well known historical personalities as blonde. In addition, 250 individuals are recorded to have had the name Flavius, meaning blonde, and there are many named Rufus and Rutilius, meaning red haired and reddish haired respectively The following Roman gods are said to have had blonde hair: Amor, Apollo, Aurora, Bacchus, Ceres, Diana, Jupiter, Mars, Mercury, Minerva and Venus.*
>
> **"According to legend, the foundation of Rome took place 438 years after the capture of [north-west Asia Minor], Troy in 1182 BC, according to Velleius Paterculus (VIII, 5).**"[39]

Centuries later, the Zoroastrian civilization of ancient Persia (Iranian *Achaemenid* Empire) took up the military mission where the ancient Turks had failed to prevent

---

[39] http://en.wikipedia.org/wiki/Founding_of_Rome

White People

Caucasians from running roughshod into central Asia, thus they crossed the Dardenelles. In any event, Persia did continue using the symbol of the wing one, which meant: *"God takes to battle against the devil"* in their role of combating the more savage Scythian ethos.

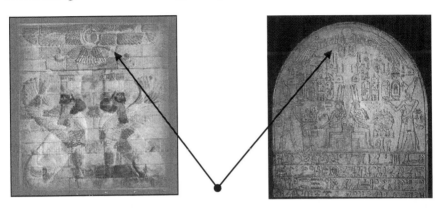

Persian king Darius Symbol of winged ones   Egyptian king Ahmose symbol of winged ones

This symbol represents the form in which God takes to battle against the devil.

As you can see Darius the Great employed the religious symbol of the winged one and the Cherubim. It was borrowed from ancient Egypt.

So I say again, once upon a time when ancient Persia governed the Biblical lands under Zoroastrianism, their mission was to not only maintain civil obedience, but also keep Europe's fierce tribes out of the civilized cities of the righteous. The reason was: Caucasians were not yet ready to rule themselves, let alone the religious order and global politics. But their time was fastly approaching.

In 330 BC, after the Greco-Persian Wars under Alexander the Great, Greek city states finally collapsed Persia's monotheistic empire. This war represented the breaking of Moses' civilization for the *people of the book* as well as the white race's rejection of monotheism and all pantheon gods in the likeness of black mankind. In effect, Moses' civilization lasted 1,700 years (4000 BC to 330 BC) until it was finally broken by Alexander the Great. Yes, this heathen-warrior broke the civilization of Moses. Rather than monotheism, Hellenism would dominate the mind of white mankind.

Nimrod Married His Mother

Moses' civilization had been under attack and/or was resisted by many Caucasian tribes of Europe as early as 4,000 BC. The first major adversary was the Caucasoid Assyrian Nimrod—a mysterious vile man born between 4000-3100 BC.

> *"Nimrod married his mother Ester when Moses (Mossa) was sent to the devils 4,000 years ago. This meant the end of the Blackman's power to keep them in their boundaries of Europe. This brought them out of the caves putting them on the road to the conquest of Asia, (Black, Brown, Red and Yellow man). Nimrod killed his father and began sleeping with his mother, Ester, known today as the holiday called Easter. She had children by her son Nimrod, making Nimrod his own father and son, which was the beginning of the lie that God and son are one And the same. It's true that this made Nimrod, his own father but the father and the son could never be identical. This is also where the lie originated of the 'Immaculate Conception' woman giving birth without the agency of man.*
>
> *"Nimrod and his mother were worshipped by the people, and knowing that if they found out that she was bearing her son's children they would not respect her, she lied telling the people that the spirit was visiting her, giving her babies. The people, being paganish, believed those lies thus establishing a holiday called Easter commemorating her birthday. They used the sign of the rabbit, which is an over-sexed animal; and eggs representing the first stage of the "embryo" chicken, which is capable of laying eggs without a male, was also used.*
>
> *"Nimrod would go into Asia robbing the brothers of their wealth. Using his unalike attracting power, he was able to steal and divide the brothers. The cross-originated as a symbol meaning death and dividing the four brothers, so that*

Nimrod could rule. The cross is used in most European nations today in their flag in the same form.[40]

When year 330 BC arrived, <u>Greek city states</u>, after the <u>Greco-Persian Wars</u> under Alexander the Great, finally collapsed Persia's monotheistic empire. This war represented a) the breaking of Moses' civilization and b) the white race's rejection of the cosmological order of the original Black world. {Holy Quran 18:20} *'If they discover you, they will stone you, or force you to revert to their religion, then you can never succeed".* By the time members of the original nation discovered who the white race really were, it was too late. Resistance was futile. The battle was like infantilism vs. cunning and cunning won through tricks, lies, divide and conquer.

In effect, Moses' civilization lasted 1,700 years until it was finally broken with the birth of Alexander the Great and his Greek army. But even before this pagan-warrior, the civilization of Moses had been under attack and/or was resisted by many Caucasian pagan tribes.

Nimrod was the first major adversary to oppose Moses' civilization. To trace down his mysterious history, start with the Uruk period. Nimrod is also named Ninurta or Bel-Marduk. Both he and his sex crazed mother/wife, Inanna or Semiramis—the queen of Babylon, are shrouded in mystery and legend. With more research you will discover how Nimrod and his mother's inversion of the truth not only creept down into Roman and Greek theology, but Jewish Talmudic beliefs too, which lead to the invention of Christianity—a religion Europe's fierce tribes finally accepted and one by which the white world uses to subject and influence Black America to except outright racism with a smile.

In all fairness, had this particular religion, Christianity, not been invented and revised by its Jewish religious

---

[40] www.muhammadspeaks.com/Nimrod.html

predecessors, Europe's most rebellious and pagan tribes; the *Jutes, Angles, and Saxons*—Northern Europeans would not have been redeemed to help European Jews rule civilization along with their gentile brethren. (See illustration of Nimrod on page 80)

The Honorable Elijah Muhammad revealed Nimrod under these terms:

> "Nimrod married his mother Ester when Moses (Musa) was sent to the devils 4,000 years ago. This meant the end of the Blackman's power to keep them in their boundaries of Europe. This brought them out of the caves putting them on the road to the conquest of Asia, (Black, Brown, Red and Yellow man). Nimrod killed his father and began sleeping with his mother, Ester, known today as the holiday called Easter.
>
> "Nimrod would go into Asia robbing the brothers of their wealth. Using his unalike attracting power, he was able to steal and divide the brothers. The cross-originated as a symbol meaning death and dividing the four brothers, so that Nimrod could rule. The cross is used in most European nations today in their flag in the same form.

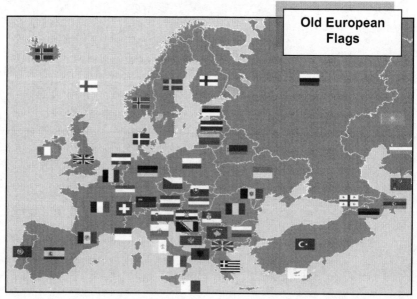

Old European Flags

> "...They didn't want the Blackman's religion, Islam, nor would they accept the Yellow man's religion, Buddhism, the white man had to invent himself a religion that would fit his nature, for his being evil, his religion had to be flexible enough to allow him to practice his evil and worship statues, drink blood (wine), eat (body flesh), etc. They applied the teachings of Moses (Islam) to paganism, thus Judaism began. Judaism kept the Jews a united people. The other devils used parts of Judaism, paganism and combined all those teachings together, thus began Catholicism, out of Catholicism they invented Christianity 551 years ago.
>
> "We wouldn't expect a white man to accept a Black, Brown, Red and Yellow man's religion. They hate everything Black...That stands for Black....Judaism is a mixture of Moses teachings, Islam, and paganism to make it more flexible....
>
> "Nimrod is mentioned in the Bible (Old Testament) as a mighty, mighty hunter in opposition to God. This is because he turned against the teachings of Moses. Nimrod was a white man who was born 300 years before Christ. He took the teachings of Moses and used them as a game to set up the early pagan Empires such as Greece and Rome.
>
> "There is more to this but I will not include it now. Just like Alexander the Great, Nimrod went among the original people to divide and rob them of their wealth."[41]

Alexander the Great was a Greek. The religion he perpetuated around the ancient biblical world was Hellenism. Today one might say *Democracy*, and *Globalization*. Either way, it means divide the original habitants of their land, rob them of their resources and takes as much wealth on the cheap as possible. This practice has been the white man's way over the past 6,000 years. We know from history since 330 BC and prevalently since 1492 when Columbus

---

[41] http://www.muhammadspeaks.com/index2.html

discovered America. Therefore, Quran says, *"Shall We [نَحْنُ nahnu] treat those who believe and do good works as those who spread corruption in the earth; or shall We treat the pious as the wicked?" (Quran 38:28)*

Image of Nimrod

The Book of Jubilee mentions the name of **"Nebrod"** (the Greek form of Nimrod) only as being the father of Azurad, the wife of Eber and mother of Peleg (8:7).[42]

---

[42]Other suggested research can be found at **www.americanpresyterianchurch.org/objects%20of%Worship.htm**.

Nimrod was a king, a mysterious vile Babylonian ruler born between 4000-3500 BC. He even replaced himself in the stead of a more ancient god named Assur also symbolically  represented to your right, as The Winged Ones. Again, notice how Assur is presented like the *"winged ones"*, which means, I reiterate, the god of war, the omniscient king. Assur was venerated by an original black people in Babylonia before they were overruled by invading Caucasian tribes.

Notice the *"winged ones"* symbol shown above, with some figure[s] residing within an apparent craft in the sky. Then see two figures seemingly making supplications beneath. Well this message was prepared by a 5,300 year old Sumerian settlement around Babylonia. Sumerian means *"the black-headed ones."* Their image-writing speaks volumes regarding future events. So the questions were:

which one will survive the War of Armageddon, God's people or the people of the Devil?

Around 2,400 BC, the Sumerians began to lose control over their territory to the Akkadians, a Semitic-speaking group of people, who soon dominated the region of Sumer. By 2,000 BC the entire region was conquered by Amorites (West Semitics).[43] It may be these west Semitic people who were also affiliated with the Assyrians.

"The Assyrians were Semitic people living in the northern reaches of Mesopotamia; they have a long history in the area, but for most of that history they are subjugated to the more powerful kingdoms and peoples to the south. Under the monarch, Shamshi-Adad, the Assyrians attempted to build their own empire, but Hammurabi soon crushed the attempt and the Assyrians disappear from the historical stage. Eventually the Semitic peoples living in northern Mesopotamia were invaded by another Asiatic people, the Hurrians, who migrated into the area and began to build an empire of their own. But the Hurrian dream of empire was soon swallowed up in the dramatic growth of the Hittite empire, and the young Hurrian nation was swamped. After centuries of attempts at independence, the Assyrians finally had an independent state of their own since the Hittites did not annex Assyrian cities.

"Beginning with the monarch, Tukulti-Ninurta (1235-1198 BC), Assyria began its first conquests, in this case the conquest of Babylon. The Assyrian dream of empire began...[44]

Moses' Temple Attack

On October 22, 2005 *CAIS ARCHAEOLOGICAL & CULTURAL NEWS* reported the discovery of a 3000-year-old temple in Iran's West Azarbaijan Province, which they believe is the long-lost Temple of Musasir. The city of

---

[43] http://www.eridu.co.uk/Author/myth_religion/sumerian.html
[44] http://wsu.edu/~dee/MESO/ASSYRIA.HTM

Musasir is located near between the Black Sea and Caspian Sea, just south of Lake Urmia shown on map 12.

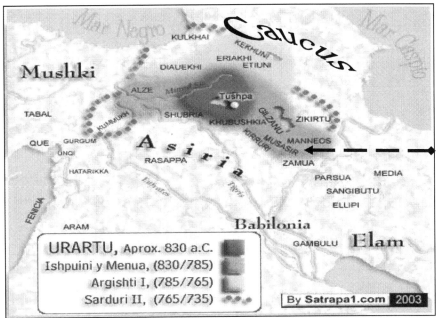
Map 12

Image A is an illustration of the Temple. (Also see similarities between temple and White House center design).

Image A

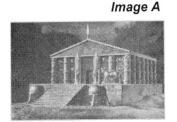

Scholars also say the Musasir Temple was captured and plundered by Sargon II of Assyria in 714 BC enduring until it fell to the Assyrian empire in 722 BC. The image below is an Assyrian bas-relief from Khorsabad (Dur

Sharrukin) depicting their destruction of the Musasir temple as shown below.

Notice the name **Musasir** contains the word **Musa**, the name of the prophet whom Elijah Muhammad revealed was sent to Caucasians to put them on the road to civilization? Ancient artifacts discovered at Musasir and its surrounding regions (Southern Transcaucasus), particularly ancient Armenia *"Sacsina"*, heavily reflect ancient Egyptian culture. It may be at this religious center in central Asia where Caucasians gathered and were taught how to conduct themselves by applying religious gesticulations and rites in honor of prophet Mossa (Moses or Musa)—their liberator.

Essentially, the people of Musa (Moses) were/are protecting their world order against the most barbaric cultural norms of the Caucasian race or Caucasoid peoples who live by the tutelage of Talmudic doctrine or influence. Hence, today, the White House is their last residence of power to uphold the rule of law under Caucasian authority, not God's authority.

Subsequently, the original nation has been misused in the clashes between "Caucasoid" civilizations for many centuries now as an old world goes out and a new world is coming in to replace it.

www.armenianaryans.com/AC/showthread.php5?p=2067

EIGHT
Skunk Of The Planet Earth

Skunkha, the Scythian king was defeated in 520/519 BC according to the concluding inscription written on an ancient monument in Iran by the Persian king Darius who stated "Scythians wear pointed caps." The monument further states the following words wherein King Darius says:

Skunkha

"Afterwards with an army I went off to Scythia, after the Scythians who wear the pointed cap. These Scythians went from me. When I arrived at the river, I crossed beyond it then with all my army. Afterwards, I smote the Scythians exceedingly; one of their leaders I took captive; he was led bound to me, and I killed him. Another chief of them, by name Skunkha, they seized and led to me. Then I made another man their chief, as was my desire. Then the province became mine.

"King Darius says: Those Scythians were faithless and Ahuramazda was not worshipped by them. I worshipped Ahuramazda; by the grace of Ahuramazda I did unto them according to my will."[45]

The pointed hats worn by the Scythians mentioned from king Darius's account reminds one of the pointed hats worn by KKK members in America. As many know, the KKK is a white Christian organization, exalting the Caucasian race and teaching the doctrine of white pride.

In 1915, a movie directed by D. W. Griffith called **The Birth of a Nation** (also known as **The**

---

[45] http://www.livius.org/sj-sn/skunkha/skunkha.html

Clansman), was presented to the U.S. public. Set during and after the American Civil War, the film was based on Thomas Dixon's *The Clansman*, a novel and play. It was the first Hollywood "blockbuster" movie but it provoked great controversy for its treatment of white supremacy portraying the Ku Klux Klan as Heros. In effect, the movie justified black mistreatment, disenfranchisement and murder.

Hooded Klansmen catch Gus, a black man whom the filmmaker described as "a renegade, a product of the vicious doctrines spread by the carpetbaggers." Gus was portrayed in blackface by white actor Walter Long.
[*Source: http://en.wikipedia.org/wiki/The_Birth_of_a_Nation*]

"*After The Birth of a Nation (1915) was released and criticized as being racist, Griffith was very hurt. He decided to make Intolerance: Love's Struggle Throughout the Ages (1916) as a follow-up, to show how damaging and dangerous people's intolerance can be. On May 26, 1918, he was elected president of the Motion Picture War Service Association, an organization charged with boosting war bond sales. Was named an Honorary Life Member of the Directors Guild of America (DGA) in 1938. The DGA award for best lifetime achievement was named for Griffith in 1953. However in 1999, television director and DGA president Jack Shea persuaded the DGA National Board, to rename the award without consulting its membership, due to the "intolerable racism" in Griffith's The Birth of a Nation (1915), even though producer H.E. Aitken, Louis B. Mayer, and many other producers invested and profited from the film which helped fund their vast motion picture empires in Hollywood."*[46]

Notwithstanding, the spirit and mindset of the KKK continues to exist among Caucasians in high places and local places in America and throughout the world. They do not want to see Black people economically, institutionally, judiciously nor politically established. It is as if they by nature, in their DNA, hate the idea of BLACK INDEPENDENCE!

Aside from this, the idea of white supremacy is at its wits end trying to maintain their pseudopigraphic Biblical Israelite-stock concept over the world. But what energy or force has kept them from achieving their ends toward accessing the proverbial "tree of life"?

"We (Black Man) did not make the white race (mankind) to be our equal in such matters as the secrets of God's Wisdom Displayed billions and trillions of years ago. If we had given the white race the original brain of the Black Man, the white race would be our equal, as the Bible gives us a hint of the race of mankind to **"drive him out of the garden lest he put forth his hand to the tree of life and live forever.'"**

"The Tree of life that lives forever is the Wisdom and knowledge of God, The Creator. For He is the Only One that Lives Forever." [47]

So I reiterate, this is why the Biblical Genesis 3:24 reads, *"So he sent the man out; and at the east of the garden of Eden he put winged ones and a flaming sword turning every way to keep the way to the tree of life."* This

---

[46] http://en.wikipedia.org/wiki/Obadiah#The_Prophet_Obadiah
[47] http://www.muhammadspeaks.com/TheShaking.html

same verse is also written this way, *"And he cast out Adam; and placed before the paradise of pleasure Cherubims, and a flaming sword, turning every way, to keep the way of the tree of life."* The True Divine Stewards of Time were no fools. Of course, they nurtured white rule 6,000 years ago, but they did not give them Supreme Wisdom that would have enable the Adamic civilization to defeat God in the final battle in the sky. *"And certainly We [نَحْنُ nahnu] created man, and We [نَحْنُ nahnu] know what his mind suggests to him -- and We [نَحْنُ nahnu] are nearer to him than his life-vein." (Quran 50:16)*

Battle In the Sky

Earlier in this book it was mentioned why and how might a great war ignite if modern day Iran is crumbled as a nation. We also know from news reports that the state of Israel threatens to destroy Iran if it continues its nuclear program.

Inspite of the public display of animosity and antagonism between many governments today, ironically they are all under to the watchful eye and/or control of one central military industrial complex. The term 'military-industrial complex' (MIC) was made famous by President Dwight D. Eisenhower in his 1961 farewell address.

In 1972 Carroll W Pursell author of *The military-industrial complex* wrote: **"Military-industrial complex (MIC)** is a concept commonly used to refer to policy relationships between governments, national armed forces, and industrial support they obtain from the commercial sector in political approval for research, development, production, use, and support for military training, weapons, equipment, and facilities within the national defense and security policy. It is a type of iron triangle."

"The term is most often played in reference to the military of the United States, where it gained popularity after its use in the speech of President Dwight D. Eisenhower, though the term is applicable to any country with a similarly developed infrastructure. It is sometimes used more broadly to include the entire network of contracts and flows of money and resources among individuals as well as institutions of the defense contractors, The Pentagon, and the Congress and Executive branch."

I began this book by stating: *"The white race was a great race of warriors."* More directly the specific tribes I was referring to were once known as Jutes, Angles, and Saxons. The term Anglo-Saxon originally meant English-speaking whites regardless of their religion or ethnicity. Their manhood training revolved around warfare. These particular tribes invaded what is now called England from Northern Europe—the geographical head of the dragon by its contour of its landmass. (See map below) Moreover, these old tribes

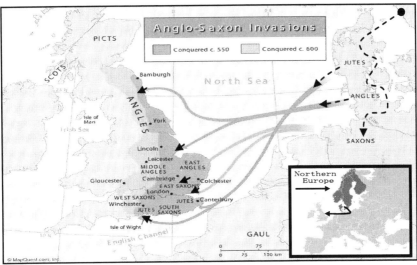

of Europe according to genetic science contain the least amount of genetic Halpogroup A & B material from the original Black nation.

What I find most fascinating is that Anglo-Saxon's folklore hero-god is named Odin, the mythological organizer of the Ossetia tribe of the Ancient Caucus Mountain's and king of old Europe's pagan tribes. Odin Rather than wander south into Central Asia, he took his tribe west and then north all over Europe building an army. In fact, Wednesday (Wodan) is named after him.

> **"Odin** (from Old Norse Óðinn) the king of the Aesir and the ruler of Asgard, is considered the chief god in Norse paganism. Homologous with the Anglo-Saxon Wōden and the Old High German Wotan, it is descended from Proto-Germanic ***Wōđinaz** or ***Wōđanaz**. The name Odin is generally accepted as the modern translation; although, in some cases, older translations of his name may be used or preferred. His name is related to ōðr, meaning "fury, excitation", besides "mind", or "poetry". His role, like many of the Norse gods, is complex. He is associated with wisdom, war, battle, and death, and also magic, poetry, prophecy, victory, and the hunt.[48]

Over the past 600 years (from England and her American Anglo Saxon offspring), 9/10th of the original nations of the earth have been geo-politically conquered. These were the people whom the ancient of days promised to give 6,000 years to rule over all living things, including their own aboriginal people of the earth.

> "ANCIENT OF DAYS is a phrase used in Daniel 7:1 to describe the everlasting God. Ancient of days literally means "one advanced in (of) days" and may possibly mean "one who forwards time or rules over it."[49]

During our modern times, the *illuminated men and women* of the Caucasian civilization are not preparing to necessarily fight a government on earth whom they also provide military weaponry and technology. Its ultimate goal is to war against the **Ancient of Days** in a battle in the sky! Their scientist of warfare, finance and religious scholarship understand the ultimate battle is going to be an aerodynamic battle against those ancient beings that represented their

---

[48] http://en.wikipedia.org/wiki/Odin
[49] http://www.studylight.org/dic/hbd/view.cgi?number=T329

power as **"winged ones"**. Cauc-asia men of war and science encountered these symbols 4,000 years ago while invading ancient Sumerians, ancient Egyptians, and ancient Persia. However, today they have yet to build crafts to win the final battle in the sky, though they are spending billions on pilot programs.

In times past, a Biblical priest named Ezekiel wrote about this future battle in sky between the Ancient of Days and the enemy of God's earth and aboriginal people. Ezekiel's text was comprehended by the religious Jewish scientists of Babylon between 595-573 BC. Of course, Ezekiel's original text was revised and now reads as follows:

> *"**4.** And I looked, and, behold, a stormy wind came out of the north, a great cloud, with a fire flashing up, so that a brightness was round about it; and out of the midst thereof as the colour of electrum (alloy of gold and silver), out of the midst of the fire. **5.** And out of the midst thereof came the likeness of four living creatures. And this was their appearance: they had the likeness of a man. **6.** And every one had four faces, and every one of them had four wings. **7.** And their feet were straight feet; and the sole of their feet was like the sole of a calf's foot; and they sparkled like the colour of burnished brass (Black). **9.** their wings were joined one to another; they turned not when they went; they went every one straight forward. (Ezekiel 1:1- 14; 24-26)*

Before reading further, I advise you to review the images on page 56 to see figures described in verse 5 and 6 above.

> *"**10.** As for the likeness of their faces, they had the face of a man; and they four had the face of a lion on the right side; and they four had the face of an ox on the left side; they four had also the face of an eagle. **11.** Thus were their faces; and their wings were stretched upward; two wings of every one were joined one to another, and two covered their bodies. **12.** And they went every one straight forward; whither the spirit was to go, they went; they turned not when they went. **13.** As for the*

likeness of the living creatures, their appearance was like coals of fire, burning like the appearance of torches; it flashed up and down among the living creatures; and there was brightness to the fire, and out of the fire went forth lightning. **14.** And the living creatures ran and returned as the appearance of a flash of lightning...**16.** The appearance of the wheels and their work was like unto the colour of a beryl; and they four had one likeness; and their appearance and their work was as it were a wheel within a wheel. **24.** And when they went, I heard the noise of their wings like the noise of great waters, like the voice of the Almighty, a noise of tumult like the noise of an army; when they stood, they let down their wings. **25.** For, when there was a voice above the firmament that was over their heads, as they stood, they let down their wings. **26.** And above the firmament that was over their heads was the likeness of a throne, as the appearance of a sapphire stone; and upon the likeness of the throne was a likeness as the appearance of a man upon it above...

The winged one's symbol as mentioned by Ezekiel 2,500 years ago is now used by Western aerodynamic military pilots and scientists as shown below. **Of course, their winged one symbol's are borrowed from the Ancient of Days—the Original black nation of the Gods.**

And so by employing these ancient symbols, the Military-industrial complex is signifying *"the God who takes to battle against their enemy."*

Between 1934 and 1975, the Honorable Elijah Muhammad revealed the reality of what Ezekiel anticipated with respect to the vision he had seen. So rather than refer to the military craft and its inhabitants that Ezekiel refers to as a wheel, Elijah Muhammad called it *"The Mother Plane"* and described it from A to Z in the following bullet points:

- The Mother Plane is made of the finest steel in Asia.
- It was made on the Island of Nippon (Japan) in 1929, and also took flight that same year.
- Black, Brown, Red and Yellow Scientists built the Mother plane.
- The Scientists did not know what they were building. [Each division built their part separate from the other]
- Her size is Half-mile by Half-mile square. Her shape is oval. Her position is 40 miles out from the Earth's sphere. She holds this position from 6 to 12 months at a time. When this time is up, the Mother Plane comes into the atmosphere of the Earth; it projects huge suction pipes out into the atmosphere to take in fresh air for our Brothers inside, then she retakes her position.

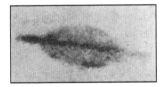
1958 Brazilian Navel Photo Shot

Location Unknown

- Her speed is up to 9,000 miles per hour in any direction, up or down, to or fro, in any direction without making a complete directional turn.
- Her contents are 1,500 small circular planes, as the devil calls them, "FLYING SAUCERS."
-

Israel

Location Unknown

Mexico

These small planes carry three (3) bombs each; they also shoot flames of fire.

- The Black men who pilot these small planes have been taught from the age of six that they are to do a special job.
- These pilots can hit any spot in America, blindfolded, as the Devil will soon see.
- The bombs that the small planes contain weigh two tons each.
- They are designed to drill into the earth upon contact, and drill from one (1) to six (6) miles through stone and rock and to explode, destroying civilization or any living matter (or life) within a fifty (50) mile radius.
- After these bombs explode, a poisonous gas is found to snuff out the remaining life, if any still exists.
- The purpose of the Mother Plane is to destroy the most wick place ever to be on the planet Earth at any time (**America, the Great Mystery Babylon**).
- At the dropping of the bombs, the flames will reach twelve (12) miles, in all directions.
- When the Destruction comes, America will burn 390 years and take 610 years to cool off.
- The Great **Mystery Babylon (America)** will perish in the flames of fire. Allah will even cause the air in which we breathe to ignite along with the atmosphere.[50]

The above words were written in the Christian Book of Revelation, namely, Rev. 13 – 19. The difference is that the Honorable Elijah Muhammad demystified the English King James Bible version. So I reiterate, how far will *illuminated Caucasians* reach to contain their form of economy and rule of law? Are they willing to battle against the Ancient of Days who would be prepared (according to Revelations 20 – 21), and now have been prepared to usher in a New World Reality by uniting the Islamic people on earth, more advanced than it was in the beginning, to replace the

---

[50] http://www.muhammadspeaks.com/MotherPlaneList.html

Caucasians juvenile rule of law and one world order concept? The facts remain to be seen but one U.S. President did publicly announce how and why the machinations of a small number of Caucasian men and women vying for a white dominated "one world order" is nearly complete and must be implemented now! He said:

> "We stand today at a unique and extraordinary moment. The crisis in the Persian Gulf, as grave as it is, also offers a rare opportunity to move toward an historic period of cooperation. Out of these troubled times; our fifth objective -- **a new world order** -- can emerge: a new era -- ...
>
> "Our ability to function effectively as a great power abroad depends on how we conduct ourselves at home. Our economy, our Armed Forces, our energy dependence, and our cohesion all determine whether we can help our friends and stand up to our foes. For America to lead, America must remain strong and vital. Our world leadership and domestic strength are mutual and reinforcing; a woven piece, strongly bound as Old Glory. To revitalize our leadership, our leadership capacity, we must address our budget deficit -- not after election day, or next year, but now." [President George Herbert Walker Bush from the National Archives September 11, 1990[51]]

Whether the leader of the Caucasoid **"new world order concept"** be black or white, it is not the New Reality that was prophesied to come and is now prepared for those who survived the fall of America and the western world's present course of actions.

> "The war is building and the four great judgments that God is going to use are rain, hail, snow and earthquakes. If you look at the weather, you already know that something is going on. When it rains, its unusual rain that comes down in torrents. It is interfering with the foundation of the houses, tearing up the streets and the roads, upsetting the railroad tracks.
>
> "The final thing is the destruction. **The Honorable Elijah Muhammad told us of a giant Motherplane that is made like the**

---

[51] http://www.sweetliberty.org/issues/war/bushsr.htm

universe, spheres within spheres. White people call them unidentified flying objects (UFOs). Ezekiel, in the Old Testament, saw a wheel that looked like a cloud by day but a pillar of fire by night. The Hon. Elijah Muhammad said that that wheel was built on the island of Nippon, which is now called Japan, by some of the original scientists. It took 15 billion dollars in gold at that time to build it. It is made of the toughest steel. America does not yet know the composition of the steel used to make an instrument like it. It is a circular plane, and the Bible says that it never makes turns. Because of its circular nature it can stop and travel in all directions at speeds of thousands of miles per hour. He said there are 1,500 small wheels in this mother wheel, which is a half-mile by a half-mile. This Mother Wheel is like a small human built planet. Each one of these small planes carries three bombs.

"The Honorable Elijah Muhammad said these planes were used to set up mountains on the earth. The Qur'an says it like this: We have raised mountains on the earth lest it convulse with you. How do you raise a mountain, and what is the purpose of a mountain? Have you ever tried to balance a tire? You use weights to keep the tire balanced. That's how the earth is balanced, with mountain ranges. The Honorable Elijah Muhammad said that we have a type of bomb that, when it strikes the earth a drill on it is timed to go into the earth and explode at the height that you wish the mountain to be. If you wish to take the mountain up a mile, you time the drill to go a mile in and then explode. The bombs these planes have are timed to go one mile down and bring up a mountain one mile high, but it will destroy everything within a 50 square mile radius. The white man writes in his above top-secret memos of the UFOs. He sees them around his military installation like they are spying.

"That Mother Wheel is a dreadful looking thing. White folks are making movies now to make these planes look like fiction, but it is based on something real. The Honorable Elijah Muhammad said that Mother Plane is so powerful that with sound reverberating in the atmosphere, just with a sound, she can crumble buildings. And the final act of destruction will be that

White People

Allah will make a wall out of the atmosphere over and around North America. You will see it, but you won't be able to penetrate it. He said Allah (God) will cut a shortage in gravity and a fire will start from 13-layers up and burn down, burning the atmosphere. When it gets to the earth, it will burn everything. It will burn for 310 years and take 690 years to cool off.

"The Book of Revelation says, And the Kings of the earth who have committed fornication with her, shall lament for her when they shall see the smoke of her burning. This fire is for us. It's prepared from men and stones. Stones represent the hard-hearted people of this wicked world and for men who refuse to change and come to God.

"You are in the valley of decision. What are you going to do? Are you going to clean up your lives? I'm not asking you if you want to join me. You can if you want to. But if you are in the church, you better make the church right because Judgment is going to begin at the so-called house of God. Wherever you are, you are going to have to clean it up. Whatever we are doing that we know is wrong, we must straighten it out. But if you don't it's on you.

"I hope and pray that I have made the message clear. Thank you fore reading these few words.

As Salaam Alaikum.

[The Honorable Louis Farrakhan June 9, 1996 at Mosque Maryam in Chicago]

Appendix 1
Failure Of The Turks

It has been reputed, "This lesson comes from the Supreme Book of Wisdom owned by our Divine Messenger the Honorable Elijah Muhammad thus given to him by our prophet W.D. Fard. The Messenger teaches us that after the Devil was manufactured on the isle of Pelan (Patmos), they came back across the dessert and entered the holy city of Mecca because Yakub taught them that Mecca was their home.

"The Messenger says that they stayed amongst the righteous for six months telling lies on the righteous having them to fight and kill one another. He stated: 'That we clothed them, shelter and treated them good cause we knew them to be a mutation of the Original people and felt it was our duty to care for them. They moved freely amongst us seeking to find ground to cause trouble and confusion.'

"The Messenger says that they would go up to the Blackman and tell him a lie that his brother was messing with his wife and the other would tell the same lie. They told the Black woman their husband was untrue causing suspicion between the Original people. After a while suspicion produce distrust and lead to argument debates and naturally soon fighting and killing. The Devil was not suspected at first because they would always step in between the unrest and offer a settlement which made many believe them to be people of peace. They were soon to be discovered as being the cause of the confusion and was rounded up. We took everything from them: our book, shelter, science, food and clothing and left them with nothing but their language of telling lies and stealing. An order was set down for them to be driven across the hot Arabian dessert and out of Asia. Asia means Light.

White People

The Devils were naked and was given an apron to hide their shame for our women. **An army was ordered to drive them across the dessert into west Asia. The land of beast and caves under the leadership of General Munk Munk. General Munk Munk rode a white horse with a high power rifle and those in his army rode Arabian horses or camels. Those that was in the army was the ones the Devils had tricked and knew the Devils ways and actions well. And this is how they got them back for the hard times they received by the Devils. As they pushed westward they didn't stop day or night. If one of the Devils fell to the sand General Munk Munk ordered them to slay on the spot. General Munk Munk made them run every step of the way until they reached the first oasis, which was 1100 miles from Mecca. Allowing them to rest, eat and drink some water for they had another 1100 miles to go before they would be clear of the land of paradise.** *After reaching the second oasis the whole group of Devils was savage and acting like animals.* **General Munk Munk had covered 2200 miles and was in Turkey of what they now call Turkey. Once he let them loose they were attracted to the caves and ran wild up into the hillside: They tore off their apron and live a beastly way of life (Bible Gen. 2:25)**

"The Devil was grafted on Pelan and was put in a new Pelan called Europe (Gen. 3:23).

"**General Munk Munk told his army that they must stay in Asia Minor Turkey and guard the border to make sure don't try to enter back into the land of peace. (Gen. 3:24) General Munk Munk told his followers (army) that because they are the ones who fell victim to the Devil tricks and did kill and hurt each other they must pay for such actions by sitting down in Asia Minor and keep the Devil bottled up in the cold caves and hillsides of Europe.** *General Munk Munk gave his followers swords, every time a Devil would try to ease out of the caves off their head went. After a while the Turks use to go across the border just to take their heads.*

"Many of the Devils went deeper into the caves where they killed animals who lived there and ate them raw thus moved in their caves, the caves of the animals was not tall enough for them to stand upright so they began to bend down. After a while they got used to it and their arms began to grow to balance their back. Hair grew all over their body cause it was cold and nature cloth them with a coat of hair like the animals. The cave men ate all the smaller things found and cast their bones outside the caves where jackals or what we now call dogs lay proud for them. The bigger animal began to move closer to the caves to eat the cavemen for there was no food for them to eat. The Devils ate all the food up from the bigger animals so these became the hunter of man. The jackals who was always outside waiting for bones became the white mans best friend because every time the big beast would come near the cave they would bark warning the cave man of danger. Some Devils lived in trees and other uncivilized places. *The dog soon became one of the cave man family and now lived in-doors. The dog was to watch the caves while the man was out hunting for food.*

"The Messenger teaches the Caucasian man and woman was walking on all fours using stone tools, eating raw meat with blood running out and eating their dead. While the white man was out hunting the dogs used to lick and smell the woman's womb, which the woman liked because of its stinging sensation. She began to love the dog because of the attention it gave her while the man was away. The cave man learned the way of the dog and began to lick and suck her womb. The Messenger also added that the dog began to have sex with the woman, which was very easy for them being that the woman walked on all fours like the dogs themselves. The dogs began planting their seeds in the women causing the women to birth mutations. The Messenger says these mutations were white babies, which had tails and the color of dogs hair and eyes. Their hair was blond at first. All

White People

types of disease originated at this period, such as the common disease syphilis which comes from dogs as any doctor can tell you if he knew the American Medical Journal if the disease comes from a dog type life this tells us to ask ourselves how many of us have come to get it? The cavewoman was full up with syphilis and all kind of deadly germs, which spread and spread.

"When Musa came to the border and entered the main land he was unable to go up into the caves because filth and waste covered the land and he was unable to enter to perform his said duty. Musa had to use the pig to eat the filth and waste before he could go in.

"Note: The history of Musa shall tell you the complete ordeal of the prophet this lesson shall deal with a certain portion of history. **Thanksgiving which is a white race holiday the Messenger teach that this holiday is all symbolic to what took place in General Munk Munk time. The white man tries to trick us into believing that when he came to America they met the Indian and gave gifts. But the white man when he came to America or New World he went to look for food when they saw the turkey it reminded them of the Turks who wore red fez with a tassel hanging down their heads, which was loose meat upon the Turkey head. This is why they named the bird "Turkey". The white man would take this bird and chop off its head. It was symbolic to General Munk Munk followers (the Turks) would do to them.** *This turkey was General Munk Munk followers.*

"Asia Minor was called Turkey because the Turks that had the key locked them up in the caves and hillsides of Europe. *The Devil was not really actually lead out of the caves until 1492. The opening of the New World allowed them to come to complete rulership* [52]

---

[52] www.100megspop3.com/thesupreme3/MUNK.HTM

103

Appendix 2
List of Prophets Over Past 6,000 Years

List of Prophets sent to mankind over the past 6,000 years. Jews count was 48 males and 7 female prophets who were sent. The following list of prophets is based on the Talmud and Rashi. On pages 93-95, you'll also see list of New Testament prophets and the list of prophets as identified by the Islamic world.

Abraham	Gen 11:26 - 25:10
Isaac	Gen 21:1 - 35:29
Jacob	Gen 25:21 - 49:33
Moses	Ex. 2:1 - Deut. 34:5
Aaron	Ex. 4:14 - Num. 33:39
Joshua	Ex. 17:9 - 14, 24:13, 32:17 - 18, 33:11; Num. 11:28 - 29, 13:4 - 14:38; 27:18 - 27:23, Deut. 1:38, 3:28, 31:3, 31:7 -Joshua 24:29
Pinchas	Ex. 6:25; Num. 25:7-25:11; Num. 31:6; Josh. 22:13 - Josh. 24:33; Judges 20:28
Elkanah	I Samuel 1:1 - 2:20
Eli	I Samuel 1:9 - 4:18
Samuel	I Samuel 1:1 - I Samuel 25:1
Gad	I Sam 22:5; II Sam 24:11-19; I Chron 21:9-21:19, 29:29
Nathan	II Sam 7:2 - 17; 12:1 - 25.
David	I Sam 16:1 - I Kings 2:11
Solomon	II Sam 12:24; 1 Kings 1:10 - 11:43
Iddo	II Chron 9:29, 12:15, 13:22
Michaiah son of Imlah	I Kings 22:8-28; II Chron 18:7-27

White People

Obadiah	I Kings 18; Obadiah
Ahiyah the Shilonite	I Kings 11:29-30; 12:15; 14:2-18; 15:29
Jehu son of Hanani	I Kings 16:1 - 7; II Chron 19:2; 20:34
Azariah son of Oded	II Chron 15
Jahaziel the Levite	II Chron 20:14
Eliezer son of Dodavahu	II Chron 20:37
Hosea	Hosea
Amos	Amos
Micah the Morashtite	Micah
Amoz	(the father of Isaiah)
Elijah	I Kings 17:1 - 21:29; II Kings 1:10-2:15, 9:36-37, 10:10, 10:17
Elisha	I Kings 19:16-19; II Kings 2:1-13:21
Jonah ben Amittai	Jonah
Isaiah	Isaiah
Joel	Joel
Nahum	Nahum
Habakkuk	Habakkuk
Zephaniah	Zephaniah
Uriah	Jeremiah 26:20-23
Jeremiah	Jeremiah
Ezekiel	Ezekiel

Shemaiah	I Kings 12:22-24; II Chron 11:2-4, 12:5-15
Barukh	Jeremiah 32, 36, 43, 45
Neriah	(father of Barukh)
Seraiah	Jeremiah 51:61-64
Mehseiah	(father of Neriah)
Haggai	Haggai
Zechariah	Zechariah
Malachi	Malachi
Mordecai Bilshan	Esther
Oded	(father of Azariah)
Hanani	(father of Jehu)
Female Prophets	
Sarah	Gen 11:29 - 23:20
Miriam	Ex. 15:20-21; Num. 12:1-12:15, 20:1
Deborah	Judges 4:1 - 5:31
Hannah	I Sam 1:1 - 2:21
Abigail	I Sam 25:1 - 25:42
Huldah	II Kings 22:14-20
Esther	Esther

White People

List of New Testament Prophets

John the Baptist	James
Jesus	Simon
Peter/Simon	Judas (brother of James)
Andrew	Judas Iscariot
James	Matthias
John	Barnabas
Philip	Paul/Saul
Bartholomew	Agabus
Matthew	
Thomas	

List of Prophets and/or messengers according to the Islamic World

According to Islam, the following prophets were given a book of scripture that was left with civilization. *"These are the ones to whom we have given the Scripture wisdom and prophet hood." (Quran 6:89)*

1-Abraham (also named as a prophet in 19:41 and 33:7)

2-Isaac (also in 19:49 and 37:112)

3-Jacob (also in 19:49)

4-Noah (also in 33:7)

5-David (also in 17:55)

6-Solomon

7-Job

8-Joseph

9-Moses (also in 19:51 and 33:7) and Aaron (also in 19:53)

10-Zachariah

11-John (also in 3:39)

12-Jesus (also in 19:30 and 33:7)

13-Elias

14-Ismail (19:54)

15-Elisha

16-Jonah

17-Lot

18-Idris (named a prophet in 19:56)

19-Mohammed Ibn Abdullah (33:40)

Appendix 3
Pkharmat

The legend hero of certain Caucus Mountain tribes is named Pkharmat. It is said he brought them fire, which allowed them to forge metal, heat their homes, cook their food, thus putting a stop to eating raw meat. Legend has it, Pkharmat taught civilization to the Caucasian race. As a result of this, "their people united and became a nation." Legend says:

"Pkharmat (Creator of the nation, language or land) is a legendary hero of the <u>Vainakh</u> legend hero who brought this group fire, which allowed them to forge metal, cook and illuminate their houses. As a result of this, the people united and became a nation.... Interestingly enough, all the indigenous religious traditions with a figure equivalent to Pkharmat were practiced by <u>peoples of the Caucasus</u> and some Indo-European peoples (who sometimes resided in the Caucasus, as is the case with the <u>Armenians</u> and <u>Ossetes</u>...

"This seems to support the <u>hypothesis</u> that the original homeland of the <u>Indo-European peoples</u> lay to the immediate north of the Caucasus touching both the Black and Caspian Seas and possibly extending north along the Volga some length as well as somewhat west into Ukraine. This hypothesis is now the most widely accepted, rather than the hypotheses that the Indo-European languages originated in the Anatolian plains, in the Armenian highland, India, Balkans or the ancestral <u>Slavic</u> homelands, or that they were a sprachbund. Comparison of the various versions of the stories also support that the original Indo-Europeans probably had more intense cultural exchange with the North Caucasus than the South Caucasus—the forms most close to the

Indo-European versions of the tale are, in fact, the <u>Circassian</u> version and the <u>Vainakh</u> version.

"Interestingly enough, the Circassian and Abkhaz name for the hero is Pataraz, which shows very noticeable similarity to the Greek name Prometheus, which is similar to most other Indo-European versions; comparing these two, it is also possible to note Pkharmat's similarity. It is possible that Pataraz, Prometheus, Pkharmat and possibly others are all roots from the same original name."[53]

I will not offer any further explanation. It speaks for itself when you understand the teachings of the Honorable Elijah Muhammad.

---

[53] en.wikipedia.org/wiki/Pkharmat#Equivalents_of_Pkharmat_in_other_traditions_and_their_significance

Other Books by the Author

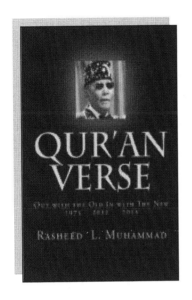
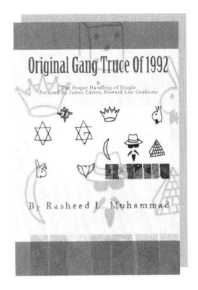
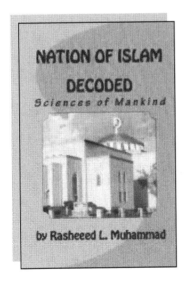

Contact 2014noiap@gmail.com

Made in the USA
Columbia, SC
06 November 2017